WHY DO I FEEL GUILTY WHEN I'VE DONE NOTHING WRONG?

WHY DO I FEEL GUILTY WHEN I'VE DONE NOTHING WRONG?

■ ■ ■ ■ ■

Ty C. Colbert, Ph.D.

THOMAS NELSON PUBLISHERS
Nashville

Published in Nashville, Tennessee, by Thomas Nelson, Inc., and distributed in Canada by Lawson Falle, Ltd., Cambridge, Ontario.

Scripture quotations are from the NEW KING JAMES VERSION of the Bible. Copyright © 1979, 1980, 1982, Thomas Nelson, Inc., Publishers.

The case histories described in this book are composites and do not describe specific individuals.

Library of Congress Cataloging-in-Publication Data

Colbert Ty Chris.
    Why do I feel guilty when I've done nothing wrong? / Ty C. Colbert.
      p. cm.
    ISBN 0-8407-7744-2 (pbk.)
    1. Guilt. 2. Shame. I. Title
BF575.G8C65   1993
152.4—dc20   92–33199
                                    CIP

Printed in the United States of America
1 2 3 4 5 6 7 — 98 97 96 95 94 93

To
my father who, through his hard work,
gave me the opportunity to think, grow, and write.

To
the abused and the children of dysfunctional families
who have come forward in the last few years,
opening their hearts and teaching my profession
about the destructive effects of guilt and shame.

Thanks also, to
my editors Darlene Hoffa,
Ron Haynes, and Jane Jones.

Contents

Preface

I became interested in the topic of guilt as I tried to understand and heal the guilt in the lives of my clients. Working with victims of child abuse, incest, and rape only intensified my desire to learn.

In 1984 I began writing a book about guilt, but finishing the manuscript became quite frustrating. Every time I attempted to edit my writing, I had gained so much new knowledge that I felt compelled to go back to the beginning and rewrite the book. I also began to realize that a fundamental difference exists between the concepts of guilt and shame. Eventually, after a number of rewrites, I had a manuscript of over four hundred pages. That's when I put the project aside, believing no one would want to wade through four hundred pages on guilt and shame.

Then one day, about six years later, I felt inspired. I sat down and began again. Six weeks later I had written this small book that summarizes all I have learned over the years about guilt and shame. Hopefully, it answers the question, "Why do I feel guilty when I've done nothing wrong?" with a practical understanding of how to avoid unnecessary guilt and heal destructive shame.

I hope it will help you to stop feeling guilty and begin to love yourself the way God intended.

CHAPTER ONE

What Is Guilt?

Guilt is a natural and valuable emotion. We must have proper concepts of right and wrong in order to function adequately in this world. Awareness of this guilt helps us to recognize and admit wrongdoing or irresponsible behavior, confess and ask forgiveness, make amends when necessary, change our behavior, and then move on leaving the guilt behind.

This behavior-correcting mechanism is an important part of the developing self and the creation of proper relationships. Ideally the only kind of guilt we should feel is a sense of remorse resulting from intentionally harmful or irresponsible behavior, and we must learn to address it properly for our own benefit. These feelings are what we call *true guilt*.

But guilt is a much more complex emotion than this explanation of true guilt seems to imply. In fact, guilt can become a devastating emotion. It can linger on and on, affecting many aspects of our everyday lives. More importantly, it is often most dangerous when we are not guilty of any wrongdoing.

Children of divorce, for example, often come through the experience of the breakup of their parents' marriages feeling guilty, as if they were somehow responsible. Children of alcoholic parents often carry the guilt and shame of their dysfunctional childhoods right into adulthood. And women who were raped, even as adults, often feel that somehow they asked for what happened to them or deserved it and, consequently, suffer with extreme feelings of guilt.

This other kind of guilt is *false guilt*. It seems to come at us like a growing cancer destroying everything in its path. It can tear at us, haunt us, follow and cripple us, leading to such severe symptoms as extreme anxiety, depression, and feelings of hopelessness. The pain of this guilt can penetrate so deeply that it can even force a person to take his life. This false guilt can possess us to such a degree that eventually a part of us even begins to seek it.

A client of mine who was tormented by guilt wrote this poem.

> It is very important for me to feel bad.
> If I feel bad then that proves how rotten and crummy
>   my life really is.
> For some strange, odd reason that is what I want.
> To be deprived of liberty—
>   That is what I want.
> To be chained to hell—
>   That is what I want.

And I don't know why.
I just don't know why.
Something a long time ago made me resist growth.

What bothered me most about this poem, or rather the emotions it expresses, was that the individual who wrote it had lived a very moral life. He had never been in jail, nor had he ever seriously hurt anyone. Yet, as he expressed in the poem, the guilt he was feeling was destroying his life and blocking the growth of his selfhood. Furthermore, he had reached the point of losing all control over his guilt, as if a part of him were choosing the guilt.

So what is guilt? Why is it such a mystery? Why do some people feel no guilt, enabling them to kill or harm others, while others seem forever trapped by their guilt?

ARE GUILT AND SHAME THE SAME?

As confusing as guilt may seem, it is not all that difficult to understand. Part of the problem is the lack of a clear distinction between the concepts of guilt and shame.

Even though guilt and shame often mesh themselves together to form one single emotional and cognitive experience, theoretically they can be defined as two distinctly different aspects of our emotional systems. Guilt is usually associated (both correctly and incorrectly) with a person's behavior, while shame is more closely associated with a person's selfhood or self-worth. Guilt is more a cognitive response; shame is more a feeling response.

Guilt: Did I do something wrong?
(Mind drawing conclusion)

Shame: Am I a bad person?
(Based on feelings of worthlessness
and so forth)

Guilt and shame can be separated into four kinds of emotion: *true guilt, false guilt, constructive shame, and destructive shame.*

- *True guilt* is a valuable, worthwhile emotion. It helps us recognize our inappropriate or irresponsible behaviors.
- *False guilt* is an undesirable emotion that is not caused by any wrongdoing, but is a psychological defense mechanism against pain.
- *Constructive shame* is natural in small amounts and necessary for the proper development of an individual's selfhood and conscience.
- *Destructive shame* is undesirable and is the result of being subjected to a violating world.

EMOTIONAL HEALING VERSUS EMOTIONAL ILLNESS

The illustration below is a graphic representation of the four kinds of guilt and shame, showing that both true guilt and a small amount of felt shame are necessary for the proper growth of an individual's selfhood and his relationship to others. On the other hand, false guilt and too much shame can cause emotional disorders, such as depression, anxiety, low self-esteem, and addictive and compulsive behavior.

If you are suffering from any of these disorders, there is a good chance that some unresolved false guilt and

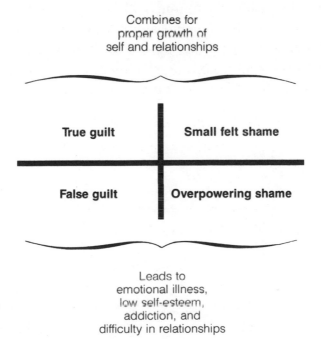

Combines for
proper growth of
self and relationships

True guilt	**Small felt shame**
False guilt	**Overpowering shame**

Leads to
emotional illness,
low self-esteem,
addiction, and
difficulty in relationships

shame are hidden beneath these disorders. Not only does false guilt combine with shame to cause these symptoms, false guilt also confuses us about what is right and wrong. As suggested by the title of this book, false guilt makes us wonder *Why do I feel guilty when I've done nothing wrong?*

The goal of this book is to help you understand and master the four emotions of guilt and shame. This will be accomplished as you correct your behavior to eliminate true guilt, learn to recognize and stay away from all false guilt, and keep the shame in your life to a bare minimum.

The next chapter defines the four kinds of guilt and shame in greater detail and will help you understand how true guilt and a small amount of felt shame help you, while false guilt and an overload of shame are destructive. In the succeeding chapters we will take an in-depth look at all four, learning how to resolve each one correctly.

CHAPTER TWO

Where Does Guilt Come From?

Most of the confusion surrounding the topic of guilt can be eliminated by simply understanding that there are four kinds of emotion involved with the feelings most people identify as guilt: true guilt, false guilt, constructive shame, and destructive shame. Most people who suffer from false guilt feel very guilty, yet they have actually done very little that is legitimately wrong. False guilt and destructive shame are their main problems. However, to correctly identify false guilt and excessive shame and know what causes them, we must first be able to differentiate between true and false guilt.

TRUE GUILT

True guilt is the remorse we should feel or recognize when we have:

- Intentionally done something to hurt or degrade another person,
- Acted in a careless or irresponsible way, or

- Intentionally broken a law or an accepted standard.

The key to distinguishing true from false guilt is whether the action was intentional. In other words, you are not guilty of any wrongdoing unless you *intentionally* chose to do something wrong.

Let's say, for example, that little Billy, age five, spilled his milk at the dinner table. Was he guilty of any wrongdoing and, therefore, should feel true guilt? To answer this question, we need to know how his milk was spilled.

If everyone at the table was having fun and Billy became a little excited and accidentally spilled his milk, he wasn't guilty of wrongdoing. It might be appropriate for someone to gently remind Billy to be more careful, but it wouldn't be appropriate to punish or discipline him.

Parents need to be careful of their responses when a child accidentally does something wrong. Billy will feel some true guilt on his own that will help him avoid future accidents. But if his parents bring on more guilt by disciplining him for an unintentional accident, his self-esteem could be harmed, particularly if they go so far as to shame him.

Suppose Billy was mad and deliberately spilled his milk. If that was the case, he intentionally chose his action and is guilty of wrongdoing. He should be held responsible, but he doesn't need severe punishment. His natural response of true guilt will help him learn to correct his behavior. His parents should gently point out that his behavior was inappropriate.

What if Billy did not intentionally spill his milk, but spilled it because of deliberate irresponsibility? (Perhaps he had set his glass too near the edge of the table, but already knew that wasn't wise since he'd had accidents that way before.) If this is the way the milk was spilled, it may be difficult for Billy's parents to resist shaming him, but Billy's behavior-correcting mechanism will cause him to feel some true guilt and help him change his behavior. Just as in the case of a deliberate intention to spill the milk, spilling it because of carelessness or irresponsibility doesn't require severe punishment. But Billy's parents will need to discipline him for his irresponsible behavior.

It is important for parents to correctly identify a child's motive and react appropriately. If the child is punished unfairly, his self-esteem will suffer. At five years of age, Billy is old enough to recognize his intentions, and his natural sense of true guilt will help him put his responsibility for the spilled milk in perspective. Severe punishment, however, will give him the message, "My milk was spilled—I'm a bad boy," and Billy will feel false guilt.

On the other hand, when a child intentionally does something wrong and does not feel a consequence, he gets the message that irresponsible behavior is okay. The lines between right and wrong become fuzzy, and if this behavior continues, he learns to block out feelings of true guilt until his ability to develop a conscience is hindered. Eventually he will lack the ability to recognize his personal responsibility for his actions, confess and ask forgiveness, make amends where needed and change his behavior, and experience healing.

A more serious example of deliberate irresponsibility is the person who drives a car when he has been drinking and accidentally kills someone. He or she did not mean to hurt anyone, but was carelessly irresponsible. Because he had a choice (to drink or not to drink; to drive or not to drive), he is responsible for his actions.

The third source of true guilt is the remorse we should feel when we have violated one of God's or society's laws. Committing a traffic violation, for example, might not cause a person to feel much guilt, but he (or she) is still guilty of breaking a law he knew he should obey. The true guilt he feels should help him change his behavior.

This very simple discussion of the three basic conditions that result in true guilt shows that true guilt is a good emotion. It rightfully brings us to the point of confession and resolution. If we have intentionally hurt someone, and if we apologize and ask forgiveness, a healing should take place in our own hearts and hopefully in the damaged relationship as well.

If a father violently lost his temper with his son, the father acted irresponsibly and the remorse he feels is true guilt. By apologizing to the son, the father will help to heal his own wound as well as the damage his outburst caused to the relationship between the two of them. If the apology is part of a resolve to monitor and control his temper, the father can eliminate his true guilt. And he will teach his son a valuable lesson about recognizing true guilt and eliminating it.

I remember a time when I helped plan a Christian weekend retreat at a nearby campground. In order to do something we wanted to do, the leadership team needed to tell a small lie to the campground management. The lie appeared so harmless that none of us thought much about it or seemed to mind it—no one, that is, except Jim. Jim calmly and non-judgmentally said he felt God would somehow honor us if we told the truth. We chose Jim's path, and the little bit of true guilt I was feeling, that I had not even recognized, turned to feelings of deep, peaceful cleansing.

I am thankful to Jim for this simple lesson, not because I believe I can live a perfect life, but because it taught me that the cleaner the life I live, the better I will feel about myself. I am thankful because as I identify and eliminate true guilt from my life, I come to love myself more completely.

At times we all fall short, hurt others intentionally, or violate some aspect of God's creation or society's laws. We are, after all, human and incapable of living our lives perfectly. But we can minimize our true guilt by attempting to live morally clean lives. I don't say this to make you feel guilty, but to help you realize that the more morally we live our lives, the better we will feel about ourselves. More importantly, we must come to understand that we can ultimately, or ideally, eliminate all true guilt with confession and forgiveness. God is both strict and forgiving. He has set the boundaries and when we cross over He forgives us when we genuinely confess and ask forgiveness.

Once true guilt has been dealt with properly, it should be gone. What should remain is a sense of inner peace and self-forgiveness. If not, then what is left is most likely false guilt.

The key concept to remember in terms of true guilt is *intention*. You are not guilty of any wrongdoing unless you acted intentionally or were purposely careless or irresponsible. But we also must be honest with ourselves. We must be willing to look inside ourselves and take full responsibility for our true guilt. The more we take responsibility for our true guilt, the more power we will have over the false guilt and shame we feel.

For example, when a couple begins to argue, both often become obsessed with the need to find fault with the other, while denying their own contributions to the problem. One of them may ultimately win the fight, at least in his or her own eyes, but the relationship suffers. A little bit of honesty can often immediately open the marriage to proper healing and understanding.

To think again of Billy and his spilled milk, we can see that his own understanding of his intentions is important in identifying his true guilt. The reaction of his parents is important, too, for if they overreact—with either harsh words that diminish Billy's self-esteem or severe punishment that harms his sense of self-worth— or if they underreact by paying no attention to Billy's intentional wrongdoing, Billy experiences pain and the seeds of false guilt are planted in Billy's mind.

FALSE GUILT

False guilt is an emotion the mind creates for a psychological reason. In its most elementary form, false guilt is a coping or a defense mechanism against pain.

For example, children are subjected to a lot of pain when their parents are fighting and threatening divorce. They feel isolated and alone. They feel the pain of their parents' quarrels. They also fear they will lose one of their parents.

How does a child deal with all this pain? Can he sit with it alone? No, the pain is too great. Can he turn it into anger? Can he go to his parents and say, "Mommy and Daddy, I am mad at you for messing up my life"?

In most cases a child doesn't have a proper way of dealing with his pain, so he turns his pain and anger into false guilt. By doing this he accomplishes two things and both are significant. He reduces the intensity of the pain and he creates a way he subconsciously hopes will control this pain in the future.

It is very difficult—in fact, it is impossible—for human beings to deal with raw feelings of hurt and loneliness. By creating false guilt, our minds isolate the feelings of hurt and loneliness and redirect the energy of these raw feelings toward guilt producing thoughts.

As a child begins to think "What did I do wrong? Where am I bad? Why am I not good enough?" the pain is not entirely removed, but it is significantly reduced.

The pain is reduced because the child's selfhood is not in direct contact with his hurt and loneliness. False guilt separates the self from these feelings.

With false guilt a child (or an adult) can also manufacture a sense of control. The game plan becomes "If I can find out what is wrong with me and correct it, then my mommy and daddy will not divorce and my pain will go away."

False guilt gives us a false sense of control, and from this false sense of control compulsive perfectionist behavior often arises. The more we use false guilt to push down the pain, the more we need to believe that by being more perfect, more responsible, and consequently more guilt-free, all future pain will be avoided.

As we compare these two kinds of guilt, we see that true guilt should lead to a release and inner peace, but false guilt is a trap. Because there was no wrongdoing, there is nothing to confess and there is no healing. False guilt, even though it immediately reduces the pain, eventually causes additional pain. It establishes a destructive cycle.

In seventh grade my first love suddenly broke up with me. Then, while I watched, she walked over a few feet and asked a friend of mine to go steady with her. Even though that's the way it was done back in the '50s, I was crushed, and I was standing there emotionally naked in front of everyone. I should have felt and been able to express my pain in the form of anger, but I was too embarrassed and too overwhelmed by the pain. Then my mind came to my rescue and started pushing the pain down, helping me to gain control by turning the pain to guilt-producing thoughts of, "What is wrong with me?" and "Why does she like him better?"

After a few hours had passed, my anger began to surface, and during the next couple of weeks my mind bounced from anger to false guilt to anger and back to false guilt. The anger was appropriate because her action was cruel, but the guilt wasn't. It was less painful for me to find fault with myself than to deal with the raw pain. That is why each of us creates false guilt to deal with an overload of pain and to attempt to control our world.

Another source of false guilt is one we may find even more familiar. When others attempt to control us or belittle us by making us feel inadequate, guilty, or bad about ourselves, the emotion we feel is false guilt.

This behavior is easy to recognize on an elementary school playground. Children, struggling with their own self-worth, will attempt to make themselves feel better by putting down or finding fault with other children. Adults usually call this "teasing" and often think it isn't important, but it can have destructive effects on a child. The child whose self-image is healthy can handle some of this, but the child whose self-esteem is vulnerable will suffer greatly.

Ministers often use false guilt in attempting to control their congregations. They intercede in place of God, asking or demanding that they, not God, be the authority in people's lives. These ministers act out of fear, insecurity, and the need for power—not love. They attempt to manipulate God's love as they hide from their own feelings. As a result, they cripple people, keeping them from developing a true understanding of God and a healthy relationship with Him.

Advertisers use false guilt to motivate us to buy certain products. They try to make us feel inadequate or incomplete if we don't have their products. They work on our feelings of inadequacy by promising us everything, including magical cures, financial success, and great happiness.

Many people have mastered the ability to unleash false guilt in us. They do it by the way they answer our questions, give us degrading looks, or project their "I'm better than you are" attitudes and body language. They never let us feel quite okay with them or about ourselves.

False guilt can be a frightening and destructive tool in the hands of people in authority. By making subordinates feel bad about themselves, individuals in authority convince those under their supervision not to trust their own judgment, but rather to blindly trust the person in authority.

When false guilt is coupled with an overload of shame, the result can be the total destruction of the selfhood.

CONSTRUCTIVE SHAME

As I said before, some shame is good, but not too much. Understanding the positive or constructive role that shame plays in our lives helps us to better understand this limit.

A growing body of evidence suggests that a natural shame response may be present at birth or definitely soon afterward. This shame response seems to be closely connected to the child's innate or natural tendency toward joy, curiosity, and excitement. The natural shame response apparently exists to help control the intensity of the child's inborn tendency to love life.

Evidence of the joy-shame response can be observed as the infant begins to recognize the faces of his parents. At first this recognition brings a sense of joy for both the child and the parents. At about three months the child attempts to interact and play with the parents. If the parents don't respond in a normal or desired way, feelings of shame can be seen on the child's face (his eyes and head lower).

This same pattern of joy, curiosity, and excitement versus shame can also be seen in the child as he begins to interact with his environment. Joy and curiosity are first experienced, followed by shame, as the child struggles to manipulate, control, and master his world.

As a result of this and other data, researchers believe this natural shame response plays a valuable role in the child's development in the following ways.

The natural shame response modulates the affect of the joy-curiosity-excitement aspect of the person.

Recently I was playing with my three-year-old nephew, Bradley. After about twenty minutes I was worn out, but Bradley was just getting started. As I told him, "No more," I could see a little bit of shame come to his face. I realized that this shame, this recognition that he needed to change his behavior, was absolutely necessary to help him regain control and calm himself. I also knew he was vulnerable at that moment. I was being fair when I asked him to respect my needs, but it was important that I avoid making him feel bad about himself as a person in the process.

A small amount of felt shame helps us to control our behavior, whether we are children or adults. If the shame is small and related only to behavior, the amount is not harmful; it produces growth.

The natural shame response helps to develop the person's identity.

The natural shame response is the main ingredient in the formation of our identities. Feelings of shame force us to look inward and discover ourselves.

If someone were to say, "Ty, I think you are out of line in the way you treat your son," I might put up a defensive wall at that moment, but I can assure you that when I reach a safe place I will spend some time reflecting upon what that person said. His comment will create a disequilibrium in me that will cause me to do some hard thinking to make sure what I am doing is correct. Felt shame is the driving force behind my need to introspect and discover if I need to change my behavior.

On a lighter level, if I am working on a new chapter

of a book and it is not going well, I feel a little bit of shame. If the shame is small, it will stimulate me to find out how to change the chapter. In this case the felt shame may be so small I am not even aware of it, but it's there. On the other hand, if my felt shame is too strong, then I might spend hours or days doubting myself.

A small amount of shame is absolutely essential to proper development of the self. Without this shame component, a child becomes hopelessly egocentric and unable to adjust in relationship to the world. He will never be able to be sensitive to the needs of others, nor will he become creative or able to properly solve problems. The ability to reflect inward is absolutely necessary for relating outward.

On the other hand, a child overloaded with shame can be so sensitive to others he is unable to focus upon himself enough to take care of himself. He will also lose the courage he needs to be creative and to tackle life's problems.

The natural shame response helps in the development of the person's conscience, giving him or her the potential to differentiate right from wrong.

This aspect of constructive shame is pretty well accepted. Without some sense of guilt or shame, it is very difficult to develop a conscience.

Some people argue there is no such thing as constructive shame—that the only type of shame anyone feels is destructive shame. I think this becomes an insignificant point once we learn to properly recognize and heal destructive shame. I tend to view shame in much the same way I think of spices we add to our food. Just a pinch of shame is often needed to redirect the mind in the proper direction. However, too much shame can destroy a person in the same way that too much spice can destroy a meal.

DESTRUCTIVE SHAME

Destructive shame is not an extension of the natural shame response, but results from living in a violating world. More precisely, it is caused by the pain that results when one human being hurts another.

The most serious forms of destructive shame result from one person intentionally trying to destroy the innocence of another person's selfhood. This kind of shame or guilt is not directed at the person's irresponsible behavior; it is an attempt to hurt or destroy the person's selfhood.

For example, when children tease on a playground, they try to attack the most vulnerable parts of a child, the parts that he cannot change. They attack his looks, his ethnic background, handicaps, or clothes, and his family's economic status and lifestyle. Adult gossip serves the same purpose—diminishing another in order to pump up the gossipers' sense of worth in comparison. On a more serious level, abuse, rape, and incest tear at the deepest and most vulnerable parts of a person's innocence.

All of us suffer a certain amount of destructive shame that we carry inside as a result of being laughed at, lied to, or violated. And we may feel destructive shame as a result of violating acts we have committed against others—the times we hurt others intentionally. But, for most of us, the deep penetrating shame we feel is caused by the violating acts of others.

Just as it is important for us to develop a clear understanding between true and false guilt, it is equally as important to understand the difference between constructive shame and destructive shame. Constructive shame is beneficial because it helps in our emotional and cognitive growth. Because constructive shame gives us the potential for introspection, it enables us to become more whole.

The effect of destructive shame is just the opposite. It is an attack on the selfhood, leaving us feeling bad, dirty, or worthless. Destructive shame destroys because it makes certain parts of us unlovable to ourselves.

For example, if we are degraded about our ethnicity or teased about our looks, we will gradually lose our ability to love ourselves in these areas.

EMOTIONAL ILLNESS

Most major psychological problems and symptoms are the result of an overload of destructive shame compounded by excessive false guilt. When a child is subjected to frequent acts of destructive shame, for example, the felt shame will begin to overwhelm his selfhood or self-love. Soon the amount of love he has for himself will not be sufficient to overpower the pain of the shame. At this point his mind will begin to create thoughts of false guilt to help push down the pain of the shame.

If key people in his life (parents, siblings, teachers, or peers) are also telling him that he is no good, then this pain and false guilt will just add to the slowly developing negative spiral. If the child is not affirmed and continues to live in a painful environment, then he will suffer more pain, which will cause him to feel more false guilt, which results in more pain and shame and even more false guilt. Over time major psychological symptoms will begin to appear. The more pain, shame, and false guilt the child feels, the weaker and more vulnerable his self will be to the violations of the outside world. He may develop anxiety, panic attacks, and a generalized fear of life to protect his wounded self from further violation. Eventually he may suffer depression. Over time suppressed anger may result in rebellious, acting out, or self-sabotaging behavior as his whole system attempts to suppress the mounting pain.

As the process continues, before long the person suffers a major loss of self. He may experience problems in making decisions, finding peace in life, and setting goals. In some cases paranoia or schizophrenia result.

However, a little bit of constructive shame experienced in a properly affirming environment leads to a child's ability to control his behavior, establish a healthy identity, and correctly deal with the true guilt in his life. Such a child should not have a major problem with false guilt because his shame is at a minimum and his sense of self is strong enough to confront unhealthy, painful situations.

It is fundamentally important for you to attempt to eliminate guilt and destructive shame from your life— not only for your emotional health, but for your happiness. In the next chapter you will learn how to recognize and eliminate false guilt.

CHAPTER THREE

How to Eliminate False Guilt

To help you begin to deal successfully with the guilt and shame in your life, I want to focus first on false guilt. Once you understand how to recognize and eliminate false guilt, the issues of shame and true guilt will be much easier to master.

Over the years I have developed a step-by-step process that I use with my clients, many of whom struggle often with guilt. These are the steps that will help you identify and eliminate true guilt and avoid false guilt.

1. Recognize the guilt and stop your mind—don't allow yourself to draw quick conclusions.
2. Identify the real source of the guilt or pain.
3. Determine whether you are feeling true guilt or false guilt.
4. If it is true guilt:
   a. Confess it.
   b. Ask forgiveness.

    c. Change your irresponsible behavior.

    d. Forgive yourself and move on.

5. If it is false guilt:

    a. Reverse the emotional process from false guilt to a little anger.

    b. Feel and release the hurt.

    c. Confront and/or correct the violating situation when necessary and possible.

The best way to learn these steps is to look at some examples.

Several years ago on election day, near the end of the day I had an emergency situation with a client. Consequently, the polls closed before I left my office for home and I was unable to stop off to vote as I had planned. The next day George, an acquaintance of mine who has the habit of trying to make people feel small, asked me who I voted for. Sheepishly I told him I had not voted. George made a critical comment and soon after we parted. About five minutes later I began to feel bad about myself. At that time I took Step One.

Step One: Recognize the guilt and stop your mind—don't allow yourself to draw quick conclusions.

I did not know why I was feeling bad or guilty, but with experience and practice I had learned to immediately stop these feelings from growing or turning to thoughts of guilt. In other words, I didn't let my mind think something like: "I am feeling bad about myself; therefore, I must be guilty of something." I stopped the process of allowing my feelings to jump to my mind, and I was ready to take Step Two.

Step Two: Identify the real source of the guilt or pain.

Because I was feeling some guilt, I knew someone or some incident had made me feel guilty. So I asked myself, "What is the source of the guilt?"

This step is very important. Most of the time when we feel guilt, we simply let our minds take off. But to correctly solve the problem of guilt, we must stop our minds and find the source. After a short time of searching, I realized that George had put me down for not voting. I was ready for Step Three.

Step Three: Determine whether you are feeling true guilt or false guilt.

To determine whether the guilt I was feeling was true guilt or false guilt, I had to slow my mind again. If I had allowed my mind to take off, it could have easily concluded, "Oh yes, I did not vote. George is right. I am guilty of wrongdoing." Instead I had to stop and ask, "Did I intentionally or purposely do anything wrong? Am I truly guilty of some wrongdoing?"

As I forced my mind to locate the correct source and ask this question, I then put myself in the proper position to determine the truth. In this case, I was not guilty of any wrongdoing. George had used this opportunity to act superior by finding fault with my behavior. I was ready for Step Four.

Step Four: If it is true guilt, confess it, ask forgiveness, and change your irresponsible behavior. Then forgive yourself and move on.

Once I reached this point, and not until I had completed the first three steps, I was ready to correct the situation. I had control over my mind, and I understood the circumstances correctly. If I had been guilty of wrongdoing or irresponsibility, then I would have proceeded to correct the situation.

Because false guilt can be such a powerfully destructive force, it is absolutely necessary that we determine just exactly what we are truly guilty of. If there is some true guilt, and it has been disposed of properly, there is no longer any reason to feel guilty. God forgives us at this point; we can also forgive ourselves. I was ready for Step Five.

Step Five(a): If it is false guilt, reverse the emotional process from false guilt to a little anger.

Since with this incident I was not guilty of any wrongdoing, my next step was to stop the guilt process from continuing any further. To do this I had to turn the false guilt into a little anger. Quietly I said to myself, "That George. He got me again. He is a nice person, but sometimes he gets out of line."

This step is very important. One way we use false guilt is to turn it to anger and then turn the anger on ourselves by internalizing it. When someone hurts us, makes our world unsafe, or puts us down, we should feel some hurt and anger. However, to avoid feeling the anger we often turn it to false guilt. To reverse the process, we must turn the false guilt back into anger. That does not mean we need to attack the person with our anger. Often the person doesn't even need to know we are angry.

Reversing the destructive emotional process taking place inside us is the key. If we just say to ourselves in a very passive way, "Oh, I guess I shouldn't feel guilty; maybe next time I won't," we will not eliminate the false guilt. The energy of the emotional part will remain, and it is this part that eats away at self-esteem and leads to shame, anxiety, and depression.

We must redirect that energy. We can even get mad at ourselves: "There I go again, letting someone dump on me." I would not do this every time, but it is one way to avoid internalizing the guilt. After the incident with George, as I expressed some anger to myself, I affirmed myself. George had disaffirmed me, and I needed to replace that with affirmation.

I must reemphasize the importance of this point, especially for those who have problems showing anger. For instance, some of us have parents who still occasionally say something to hurt our feelings. Basically they are good parents, who don't intentionally mean to hurt us. They are just overprotective or insensitive to our needs. We may not need to confront them, but we don't want the guilt either. A little silent anger ("Darn my mother") will at least stop the guilt in us. Finished with this step, I was ready for the second part of Step Five.

Step Five(b): If it is false guilt, feel and release the hurt.

Unfortunately I still wasn't through with the feelings I'd locked inside me because of George's behavior. Beneath my anger was some hurt. In order to properly heal myself, I needed to bring up this hurt and feel it.

When George put me down, I could have walked away feeling guilty or angry at him, but I did not want to continue feeling either of these emotions. I not only needed to turn the guilt to a little anger, I also needed to feel the hurt behind the anger. Once I had felt the hurt, I could heal and release it and remove the anger from my life.

It is very important to fully recognize the feelings of hurt and anger that lie below false guilt. These feelings can be greatly minimized by completing Step One as soon as possible. The faster we recognize false guilt and stop our minds, the smaller the amount of false guilt, hurt, and anger that remain for us to deal with.

I recalled the incident with George and allowed myself to experience the hurt. Then I could move on to the last step.

Step Five(c): If it is false guilt, confront and/or correct the violating situation when necessary and possible.

Steps Five *a* and *b* work as long as the incident is small or isn't repeated very often. By realizing the guilt was not real guilt and by expressing a little anger and feeling the pain, I had dealt with that specific incident properly. My selfhood had been preserved.

But what if George had continued his behavior? What if I had to work with him every day and this behavior became a daily habit? If I continued to let him get away with it, I would not be taking care of myself properly and part of me would know it. And if I allowed this abusive action to continue, eventually my self-esteem would suffer.

What would I do if his behavior continued? Ideally I would go to George and, if possible, share my hurt, but not my anger. While hurt is harder and riskier for you and me to share with the person who has caused it, it is easier for the person to receive. But if I told George about my anger, he might become defensive, which would reduce his ability to hear my pain. With that in mind, I could have approached George and said, "I am not sure you are aware of it, but when you criticized me for not voting I felt hurt. I need you to be more careful about freely judging me."

George might have tried to defend his actions by saying, "Well, you should vote." If he had, I would have needed to tell him that it is not his job to judge me unless my action is endangering him personally or he is concerned with my welfare.

Many of us avoid this kind of interaction because we fear negative reactions. The truth is that many times the other person might react defensively, but that is the other person's problem. It is still important for us to share the hurt or the anger. The other person might not acknowledge his wrongdoing, but we will feel better about ourselves.

This last step may be the hardest to implement. Perhaps you have a demeaning supervisor who often makes you feel guilty, but you are afraid that if you confront the situation you might lose your job. You may need to weigh the psychological toll this is taking on you. Many people I have counseled, after suffering under a critical person (a parent, spouse, or supervisor) come crawling into my office with extreme depression and shattered selfhoods. My recommendation is that they at least put Steps One through Five *b* into practice.

If you are in contact with a person who continually makes you feel guilty, and you don't know how to deal with the situation, I suggest that you seek some professional help. If the violating situation is not dealt with properly, you will eventually suffer deeply—both emotionally and physically.

Melissa came to me feeling guilty about the pain she was causing her mother. Melissa and her husband, Brian, had just moved to the West Coast from back East because of Brian's job transfer. Melissa's mother had been quite emotionally dependent on Melissa and since the move had called about four times a week. Each time she called, she bombarded Melissa with questions, such as "How could you leave me?" and "Why can't

Brian find a new job back here?" Melissa felt guilty about the move.

With Melissa's situation in mind, let's walk through the steps again.

Step One: Recognize the guilt and stop your mind—don't allow yourself to draw quick conclusions.

This step was difficult for Melissa, because each time I even mentioned her mother, up came the guilt. For most of Melissa's life, her mother had controlled her with guilt. I had to teach Melissa to separate her feelings of guilt (and shame) from her thinking process.

Step Two: Identify the real source of the guilt or pain.

In this example, obviously the source is Melissa's mother.

Step Three: Determine whether you are feeling true guilt or false guilt.

Melissa felt guilty because she had brought pain into her mother's life by moving—at least that is what her mother claimed. But Melissa hadn't challenged the situation to find the *true origin of the pain*.

Was the mother feeling pain because Melissa *intentionally* wanted to inflict pain? No. Melissa didn't move to purposely cause her mother pain. Melissa needed to do what she did. The mother's pain was the result of her own emotional overdependence. Since the mother was well provided for both physically and financially, Melissa was not guilty of a wrongful or irresponsible act.

If anyone was guilty of true guilt, it was the mother, because she attempted to use Melissa's love against Melissa. Instead of taking responsibility for her own insecurities, the mother tried to manipulate Melissa with false guilt.

Remember that false guilt is primarily used as a means to suppress and avoid pain. Unfortunately, at times most relationships require painful decisions. We bring pain into a child's life, for example, as we tell him that he can't have a cookie before dinner. Later we may bring tremendous pain into that child's life by putting him into a hospital drug rehabilitation program.

When the pain of tough decisions comes, we must learn to face the pain and with courage determine the correct decisions. But just because there is pain does not mean that guilt should follow.

Step Four: If it is true guilt, confess it, ask forgiveness, and change your irresponsible behavior. Then forgive yourself and move on.

In this example, Melissa was not feeling true guilt and, once she understood that, did not need to take Step Four. She could go directly to Step Five.

Step Five(a): If it is false guilt, reverse the emotional process from guilt to a little anger.

Melissa did not have to become outwardly angry at her mother, but she did need to become aware of how the guilt and shame were building inside her and overwhelming her. She needed to learn how to shut off that process. That could only be accomplished by turning the feelings to anger. At first the process was very difficult because Melissa had been conditioned all her life to feel guilt. In fact, just thinking about being angry at her mother brought up more guilt.

To get Melissa moving, I had to tell her to take her mind off her feelings of guilt and shame and just say to herself and to me, "I am angry at my mother. She has no right to make me feel bad about myself. I have a right to determine my own destiny."

Once she was convinced this would work, it began working. Each time the mother called, Melissa felt less guilt and more freedom.

Step Five(b): If it is false guilt, feel and release the hurt.

I did not want to leave Melissa with only two options—either feel guilty about the move or feel angry with her mother. By feeling some of the pain and releasing it, she would be in a much better position to also feel love for her mother. Sharing the pain that had resulted from being controlled by her mother and crying a few tears helped allow some of that pain to come up so it could be healed.

Step Five(c): If it is false guilt, confront and/or correct the violating situation when necessary and possible.

Melissa could not heal and grow if she allowed her mother to continue to act as she had in the past. After a while, when she felt strong enough, Melissa called her mother and, as gently as possible, confronted her. She said something like this:

Mom, I love you very much and I miss you, but I need to say something to you. I don't want you to make me feel guilty anymore for moving. My primary place is with Brian. If you seriously need me, I will come as soon as I can. I also need you to limit your calls to once a week.

When Melissa's mother heard this, she became angry. I had warned Melissa that she might. The mother was not about to give up control of her daughter that easily. She also had to test Melissa to see if she would follow through.

Melissa stood her ground in the next few weeks—she even hung up on her mother twice—and, to Melissa's surprise, her mother began respecting her. This felt so good to Melissa she felt freer to love her mother. She even called her mother sometimes on her own. That, in turn, made the mother feel more secure. The mother's insecurity had been the problem, but the daughter had to make the break. Once she did, she opened up the possibility for real love and honesty between them.

I have encouraged many other clients to make similar moves in their relationships with their parents. Usually the clients say, "Oh, but you don't know my mother/ father. She/he is crazy." Maybe so, but often part of a parent's craziness results from being out of control with his or her own need to control. Our best chance to love our parents, as well as ourselves, is to not allow them to make us feel guilty, but to reach out to them in honesty.

Confronting abusive or guilt producing parents can be quite a challenge, often a very scary one. So don't hesitate to seek professional help or the support of another person. At the same time, try to realize that some parents may be impossible to confront. Whatever your situation, remember that you need to do what is best to protect your own self-esteem and to keep your mind from turning pain to false guilt.

TWO WAYS TO BE SELFISH

Those of us who are susceptible to false guilt often have trouble putting ourselves first or choosing to be selfish. Yet to properly take care of ourselves, at times it is absolutely necessary to be selfish.

The problem lies in the fact that there are two ways to be selfish. One way occurs when a person, because of his self-centered needs, takes advantage of or misuses another. This kind of selfishness is wrong and usually results in the violation of another person's rights.

On the other hand, you and only you are responsible for taking care of your selfhood and your emotional health. No one else on the face of this earth has the primary responsibility of taking care of you. If you don't act selfish when necessary by setting proper boundaries and knowing your limits, eventually you will either suffocate emotionally or look to others to take care of you.

For example, parents do not always have to be available for their children. They can say, "We need some time to ourselves. Please play in your rooms." A wife can also say to her husband, "I need some help today. Will you do the laundry?"

Both men and women must learn to recognize their emotional limits and to value these limits. On the job or at home, it is all right to be selfish within responsible limits. But if we act selfish to escape responsibilities, that is irresponsible behavior. However, if our jobs are pushing us toward an ulcer or a heart attack, we don't need to feel guilty about taking care of ourselves properly.

CLOSING THOUGHTS

I hope these examples will start you toward eliminating guilt from your life. In the next two chapters we will discuss the topic of shame, and we will see that as shame grows in its intensity, it begins to take over our minds. We become more and more susceptible to thoughts of false guilt. With a propensity to feel shame, we are even more at the mercy of individuals who for their own reasons want to make us feel guilty.

We fight against and prevent the false guilt and shame they would cause us by taking control of our minds. We stop all feelings and thoughts of guilt and examine the situation. We ask ourselves, "Where is the element of intentionality?" We make the commitment to not feel guilty of any wrongdoing unless we are truly guilty.

Most of all, we must remember that no one has the right to make us feel guilty. They can accuse us of a wrongdoing—and they do have that right—but we must properly process that accusation, looking honestly at ourselves for any intentional or irresponsible behavior. Only then do we decide if a wrongful act has been committed, and *we* do the deciding.

Those of us with a tendency to quickly feel guilt must be aware of the pain hidden by the guilt. It is important to stay with the pain, for pain itself is not wrong. In fact, it is often necessary when honesty and truth are required.

Reread this chapter and commit these steps to memory. Go over them with a friend or counselor if you need further help. Appendix A has some Guilt Work Sheets that might be helpful. The first two are filled out according to the two examples used in this chapter.

If you commit yourself to going through the mechanical process laid down in this chapter, in a short time you will begin to conquer the false guilt in your life. If you experience difficulty in controlling your mind, it might well be the result of excess shame, the topic of Chapter Four.

Identifying Destructive Shame

Destructive shame can be defined as the feelings of worthlessness that result when part of the selfhood has been made unlovable or worthless by a violating act. To help explain the concept of destructive shame, assume that the illustration on page 40 represents your whole self, as defined by the individual parts of your identity (*A, B, C,* and so forth). Part *A* could represent your physical appearance; *B,* your athletic ability; *C,* your intellectual ability; *D,* your gender identity; *E,* your socializing ability; *F,* your wage earning ability; *G,* your child rearing ability; and *H,* your special interests. *I* would be other parts of your selfhood that are important to you that you need to identify yourself, such as your musical ability or your public speaking ability.

Your selfhood is actually made up of millions upon millions of parts. It is made up of everything that is you or can be associated with you. Parts of your identity, for example, are the state or country where you were born, the clothes you wear, the friends you choose, the athletic teams you like, and so forth. In addition to the parts that make up your identity, each part has a corresponding feeling attached to it that is either positive (warm) or negative (cold).

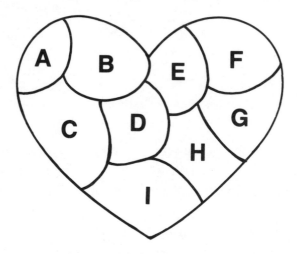

As a child if you were laughed at in the gym or always the last one chosen for a team, your physical or athletic self may feel bruised or non-affirmed, and a negative, or cold, feeling is associated with this part of your identity. On the other hand, if you were a good athlete, then you most likely have a positive, or warm, feeling about your physical abilities.

When a part of you is violated, it becomes unlovable to you, because of the pain your mind associates with that part of your identity. You can't focus on that part of yourself without feeling this pain. Because of the pain, your mind tries to dissociate, or separate, itself from that part of your identity.

Look at the figure below and let's assume that the shaded parts are the parts of the self that have been significantly violated or wounded. When a part of you is wounded, your mind will try to rescue that part and will begin to hide it from you and from the world. Your mind hides a damaged part from you to keep the hurt and shame from harming your total selfhood; your mind hides the pain from the world to prevent further injury.

For example, a young woman who was sexually abused as a child feels dirty or shameful about her sexuality. When she reached puberty she developed a compulsive desire to gain weight in an unconscious attempt to be unattractive to men. Her mind hid her wounded sexuality, because actually having sexual thoughts forced an exposure of these wounded parts and compelled her to feel the pain caused by the violations. She continues to hide this part of her selfhood, her desire for sexual intimacy, from the world by gaining weight. She might also need to hide this aspect of her life from herself by taking pride in her size or by believing she doesn't want a relationship with a man and so forth.

Describing significant violating events, such as rape or incest, helps us to understand the violating process, because it is easy to conclude that such events violate and overpower the selfhood. However, each of us has been wounded many times during our lives in less significant ways. Because our minds work hard to deny or hide these wounds, we find ourselves suffering from wounded, shamed selfhoods without much knowledge about the process involved.

To help you better understand how you may be suffering from wounded or shamed parts of your selfhood, study the diagram on page 43. Often a person is aware only that he or she suffers the symptoms given in the right-hand column. Others may not be aware of specific symptoms but may simply feel something is not right.

The first step in attempting to understand or discover the shame in your life is to assume that shame is present. If you are depressed, unhappy, anxious, or compulsive, assume that these feelings might be the result of shame your mind is hiding from you. This hidden shame is the consequence of a wounded selfhood pushed into the depths of the subconscious by your mind's ability to deny painful events or to choose not to be aware of them.

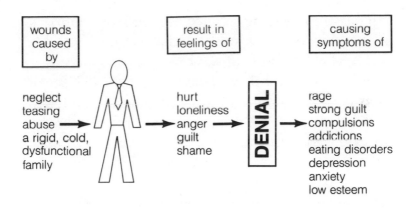

wounds caused by	result in feelings of	causing symptoms of
neglect teasing abuse a rigid, cold, dysfunctional family	hurt loneliness anger guilt shame	**DENIAL**	rage strong guilt compulsions addictions eating disorders depression anxiety low esteem

Chuck was a very talented man who, for some unknown reason, felt an inner resistance to succeeding. In therapy, as we investigated his background, we realized that he had begun to feel bad about himself when he reached a certain level of success.

As we dug deeper into Chuck's past, we discovered his father was very competitive. Even though on the surface the father seemed quite encouraging, actually he competed against Chuck. Most likely the father feared that Chuck would someday be more successful than he. Consequently during Chuck's childhood and teenage years, his father began giving small, highly disguised negative messages. Faced with the fear of losing his father's love, Chuck began believing there was something wrong with his being successful. All of this was on a subconscious level until Chuck entered therapy.

Chuck's degree of awareness of this situation is represented by the diagrams on pages 44 and 45. The conflict between wanting to succeed and not wanting to succeed was in Chuck's subconscious mind, and all he was consciously aware of was that he wasn't succeeding although he had a deep desire to succeed. The main aspects of the shame that caused the conflict were pushed down into his subconscious in order to protect his wounded selfhood.

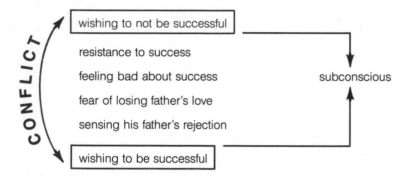

As a child Chuck needed his father's affirmation as he attempted to succeed by mastering parts of his life. When instead his father disaffirmed him, his selfhood could not handle the pain. His mind blocked out those parts of his life by denying what he really wanted. Subconsciously he felt trapped. Consciously he wanted to succeed, but subconsciously he feared that, if he did, he would lose his father's love. Therefore, on a conscious level there seemed to be two parts of him going in opposite directions: The part that wanted to succeed was working toward success, and the part that couldn't allow success was keeping him from being successful.

SUBCONSCIOUS MIND   CONSCIOUS MIND

When Chuck began therapy, he was consciously unaware of the violations he had suffered or that his selfhood had been injured. He only knew he wasn't
succeeding when he really wanted to. In therapy he
gradually became consciously aware of both the violations and the corresponding feelings and was finally
ready to be healed.

HEALING

How do we heal wounded, shamed parts? Theoretically, the process is simple: We must go back and love or
affirm the parts of our selfhoods that were made unlovable to us by violations.

Both Chuck and his employer knew he was not per-
forming up to his potential. The employer, who was
concerned about Chuck's lack of success, recommended Chuck attend a success seminar and read a
couple of motivational books.

Chuck tried these cognitive, mind re-programming

approaches. They helped some, but these methods did not remove much of his resistance. The wounded part was still injured; therefore, Chuck's mind still needed to resist.

Chuck, like everyone else, was created with a potential to be joyful, enthusiastic, and enterprising. As he attempted to exercise, or actualize, this part of his selfhood, his father disapproved instead of affirming him. The process was repeated time and time again as Chuck tried to succeed or master different parts of his world. After a few years had passed, the part of Chuck's selfhood that would allow him to be successful was severely wounded.

Desire to grow, compete, succeed, and exercise his talents

As a result, this part of his identity was shamed and made unlovable to him. In order to prevent the contamination of the rest of his selfhood, his mind blocked out as much of this shamed part as possible. The success seminar and the motivational books may have momentarily motivated his mind, because he wanted to succeed, but they did not touch the deeply embedded shame. Chuck was handicapped because this part had been made unlovable.

These cognitive, mind-altering techniques did not touch the shame, because Chuck did not have the love needed to heal this part of himself on his own. He needed his father's affirmation and unconditional love to empower him. After a certain amount of therapy, Chuck was able to uncover the nature of the violation and heal the shamed feelings, but the healing was not possible without some form of outside affirmation.

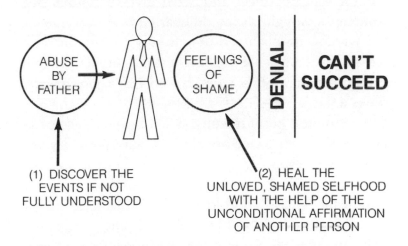

(1) DISCOVER THE
EVENTS IF NOT
FULLY UNDERSTOOD

(2) HEAL THE
UNLOVED, SHAMED SELFHOOD
WITH THE HELP OF THE
UNCONDITIONAL AFFIRMATION
OF ANOTHER PERSON

Once the shamed parts are healed, the mind automatically releases its hold on the person. In Chuck's case, he began to feel his natural desire to succeed without trying to "force himself upstream," so to speak.

The same situation may exist with a woman who was sexually abused. If she gained weight to protect her selfhood, then all the diets in the world will not work.

Her mind will still need to protect her wounded part until it is properly healed.

Leanne, a past client of mine, was sexually abused between the ages of six and seven by her mother's boyfriend. As a child she completely blocked out all of these memories. When she reached puberty, she started gaining weight, about fifty pounds over the next few years.

Leanne entered therapy—not because of her weight, but because she had been diagnosed as schizophrenic. She often heard voices and acted quite paranoid. She sometimes thought she could hear CIA officers outside her window and believed they were after her. She also felt an extreme sense of dirtiness about herself that caused her to wash her hands and her vagina several times a day.

After quite a bit of therapy, when Leanne was nearly healed, she came to me one day and said she was starting to lose weight. Up to this point in her therapy, her obesity had not been an issue because of the other more significant issues. She told me that during all of her adult life she had felt a block about losing weight, but one day she realized the block was gone.

I don't want to imply that Chuck and Leanne were healed instantly or without struggle. Both worked very hard in therapy. The point I am trying to make is that there exists in each of us, from birth, a natural desire and energy about life, but shame robs us of this desire. As a result of the violating events caused by others, certain parts of us were made unlovable. We must heal these parts before our creative-life energy can return naturally.

THE INTERACTION BETWEEN THE MIND AND THE SELF

My profession has made a fundamental error in the last twenty years or so by putting too much emphasis on the cognitive-thinking aspect of the individual's mind. When violated, the violation damages an individual's selfhood, not his mind. Our minds begin to act crazy (so to speak) after our selfhoods have been wounded.

What happens when someone you love suddenly leaves you? The wound hits you like a cannonball. Your mind takes off as a result of this violation in an attempt to help alleviate the pain. One minute your mind is intensely angry and the next minute it fills with guilt-producing thoughts, or you become extremely fearful, jealous, or anxious. In all these responses, the mind is reacting to the pain of wounds to the selfhood. It can be very helpful to "work on the mind" with cognitive, positive self-talk or verbal affirmations, but unless these methods heal the wounds to the selfhood, the healing is not complete.

Maggie grew up in an extremely verbally abusive home. As an adult she tried to protect her wounded areas by always staying in control. This method worked for her for the most part until her husband and three children began to show signs of low self-esteem and rebellion.

At this point Maggie responsibly entered therapy and began to work hard on her issues. With the help of the therapist, she was able to understand with the cognitive thinking aspects of her mind how her own dysfunctional childhood was affecting her adult life and the lives of her family. She learned how to affirm herself and her family in a positive way, and she became a much more accepting and congenial person. At this point she stopped therapy. However, in a year or two, Maggie's need for control and her need to be critical of her loved ones started working its way back to the surface.

The therapy had helped her to understand how her past affected her present. Since she was a responsible person who wanted to do the right thing, a change resulted. But the wound, which was still hidden, had not been healed. The shame, the hurt, the pain, the tears, and the anger from her wounded childhood had not been exposed and re-affirmed with love.

The positive self-talk from the earlier therapy sessions had helped. She had learned to like herself better and those around her as well. But in the end, the therapy had merely put a Band-Aid on her deeper wounds. She was stuck again, pushing her old pain down, while trying to maintain control over her environment to keep the pain in check. She was doing this at the expense of her own freedom as well as the freedom of others. Because she still hasn't dealt with her core pain, Maggie still suffers from depression, panic attacks, and a mild case of acrophobia (the fear of leaving home).

Digging out the specifically wounded areas is always necessary for healing to correctly occur. That is the only way the mind can eventually relax and allow the more severe symptoms to go away.

GUILT VERSUS SHAME

Chapter One contains a simple illustration demonstrating the difference between guilt and shame. The illustration below shows these concepts redrawn in greater depth to make the point that if a person challenges our behavior, we need to stop and determine if we are guilty of any wrongdoing. We do this by focusing on the intentionality of our behavior. If we are truly guilty, we should confess and ask forgiveness. Then we should be able to forgive ourselves without any trailing

Guilt: Did I do anything wrong? What do I need to do to correct the situation whether it is true or false guilt?

Shame: What actual part of me has been shamed, wounded, or made unlovable? What part needs to go through an inner healing to re-affirm it?

feelings of shame. If we are not guilty of any wrongdoing, we need to do whatever we can to protect our precious selfhoods.

If, after we have stopped our minds and determined whether or not we are feeling true guilt or false guilt, we cannot keep our shame to a minimum, if our minds obsess with negative thoughts about our selfhoods or we have out of control destructive behaviors, there is deeply embedded destructive shame that needs to be identified and healed.

Correctly understanding constructive shame is absolutely necessary at this point. Its purpose is simply to refocus our minds. That's all.

Suppose I say something that hurts a person's feelings. I should feel just a little shame. It will wake up my mind, so that my mind can make the necessary adjustment. Then, with minimum difficulty, I should determine the right course of action (I should be more careful of what I say and I should apologize). After I have completed the appropriate acts, my mind should calm back down and my shame should disappear (especially if the other person accepts my apology).

This small component of shame is not to be used as a punisher, but only as an indicator, or switch, to momentarily refocus my mind. As I correctly understand the situation and make the appropriate adjustments, I should feel a sense of control over my mind that removes its focus from the guilt-producing situation and places my focus back on something joyful, creative, or productive.

On the other hand, if an external situation touches a wounded or shamed part of my selfhood, I might struggle to resolve the additional guilt and shame this external situation creates. Most likely I will feel the shame at a much deeper, more painful level. The shame may make me feel worthless, dirty, or bad about myself. I may feel that I don't want to be with myself or that I don't like myself.

When my mind focuses on the shame producing external situation, I may not be able to easily make proper, quick decisions. My mind may make the situation much more complex than it is, bouncing back and forth from anger to shame to false guilt, adding many additional issues to the basic situation. And, after I've made the decision, it may haunt me for days, as I continually wonder, "Did I make the right decision?" I would feel out of control with the deep shame and the need to pound myself with guilt-producing thoughts. This would happen because old wounds diminished this part of my selfhood. I am not strong enough in this area to believe in myself. I can't make a decision affecting this part of my identity and act on it, truly believing it is the best decision I could make at the time. The diagram on page 54 demonstrates a healthy response to constructive shame and an unhealthy response to an external situation because of unresolved, shame-producing hidden wounds.

If the shame component is low, when situations of guilt arise we should be able to keep our minds focused only on our behavior. If not, then someone has wounded our personhood, limiting our potential to take care of ourselves.

Normal

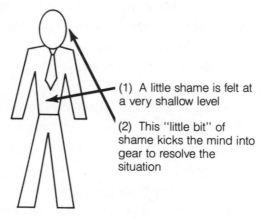

(1) A little shame is felt at a very shallow level

(2) This "little bit" of shame kicks the mind into gear to resolve the situation

(3) After the appropriate action has been taken, the mind relaxes automatically because the shame is gone

Abnormal

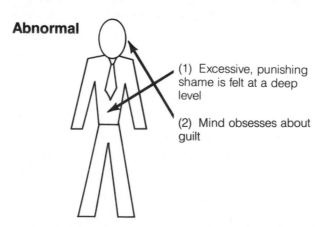

(1) Excessive, punishing shame is felt at a deep level

(2) Mind obsesses about guilt

(3) Because of deep feelings of shame there is not enough inner strength of self to make a choice or to believe in the choice. The mind and body continue to "vibrate" together, creating anxiety, depression, and the need to find relief through food, drugs, and so forth

THE DEPENDENCY FACTOR

There are fundamental differences in the proper way to heal destructive shame and the healthy ways to eliminate true guilt, false guilt, and constructive shame. We need to understand these differences very clearly.

Healing and eliminating true guilt, false guilt, and the little bit of shame that is constructive and natural simply require that we make cognitive choices. If we feel true guilt as the result of intentional or irresponsible, wrongful acts, only we can correct those situations by apologizing or doing whatever is needed. We need to use the same basic procedure when we feel false guilt. When our minds begin to create inappropriate guilt-producing thoughts, we can grab hold of them and realize cognitively that we are feeling false guilt. Using the principles explained in Chapter Three, we alone can correct the situation. No one else can do it for us, because these are cognitive choices we must make ourselves.

The only time we can't simply choose to correct these emotions is when we are overloaded with shame. Healing destructive shame is uniquely different, because an outside source of love is needed. Unlike the other three emotions that we can heal and eliminate with cognitive choices, healing shame requires help outside ourselves. We simply can't do it with only cognitive choices.

Our selfhood, our self-esteem, and our ability to love ourselves is built on the foundation of affirmation and unconditional love from outside sources. If, as children, we were not loved, emotionally nourished, and affirmed, we could not grow to love ourselves. When we were violated by major abuse, such as rape, or even a lesser offense, such as being teased about some part of our anatomies, a part of our innocence was attacked.

We were crippled by these attacks because our ability to love ourselves in these areas was removed or reduced. As a result, we became dependent on outside sources of affirmation and unconditional love to repair the wounds and remove the shame.

When Chuck was having problems succeeding, what did he need to become healed? The cognitive, self-esteem books helped him to believe in himself to a degree. But when his father hurt him verbally, he felt hurt and alone, and his mind hid these bruised parts. Cognitive choices alone did not heal his shame. What he needed most was to discover his pain and share it with a safe and supportive person. To heal, these bruised parts needed to come out and experience the love and affirmation of someone else.

The same is true of Maggie. Her acrophobia, depression, and panic attacks occur because she feels vulnerable *to* the world, not *because* of the world. Parts of her selfhood are unloved, and subconsciously she knows these parts need to be loved and affirmed by others. However, she is too afraid to expose these parts. Her solution is to try to control her loved ones, keep her anxiety down with medication, and stay at home when her anxiety becomes too high. She does all of this to keep the wounded parts that need to be affirmed and loved hidden.

All through high school I had a deathly fear of writing, and I barely passed my English classes. I don't know how it began, but I felt inadequate and shamed about my writing ability. When I was in college, I had to write a short story for one of my classes. When the instructor returned my paper, it was covered by the usual red marks, but it also contained a note praising me on how well the story was written. This one bit of affirmation filled me with so much warmth that it turned me into an enthusiastic writer. I still struggle with grammar and sentence structure, but I love to write. Every time I write something, this wounded part in me heals a little more.

People who were significantly violated or abused, especially as children, need to go through a healing process. They need to gently re-experience the wounds so the pain can come up and interface with affirmation and love. Unfortunately, those who have been extremely hurt have much hidden pain and broken trust. Consequently, the healing of these parts requires letting out the pain in the areas where the selfhood is most vulnerable.

When I share my pain of feeling inadequate with the English language, I take the chance that someone will make fun of me. But I can easily share this pain, because it is small. If I feel rejected, I have plenty of self-esteem to recover in this area, although when I was younger I didn't.

But what about a woman or man who was sexually abused as a child? The risk of sharing such events is enormous. That's why they have such resistance to letting up this magnitude of pain. Nevertheless, healing shame requires an outside source of affirmation and unconditional love. As individuals we are incapable of healing destructive shame on our own. Outside sources of affirmation are absolutely necessary.

This does not mean that the individual is absolutely helpless in the healing process. A person who feels shame from not working can find a job, and the success of the job and the paychecks he receives will be the outside source of affirmation. A person who feels shame from the lack of education can go back to school. A person who feels unloved can learn to choose relationships that are affirming and proper.

The dependency factor with shame dictates that because an outside source has disaffirmed, an outside source is needed to affirm. Outside sources can also include a spouse, a counselor, friends, support groups, a good working environment, and God. In fact, the more proper support we have surrounding us, the more chances we have to become healed.

CO-DEPENDENCY

There is a major difference between the dependency factor and the way in which people become inappropriately dependent on each other, what we call "co-dependent." To heal shame, we need the support, affirmation, guidance, and unconditional love of others. We don't need, even though most of us look for it at times, to have others rescue us from our shamed or wounded parts.

With the shame that I felt about my writing, for example, I needed the instructor to believe in me so that I could gain enough inner strength to begin healing my feelings of inadequacy about my writing ability. Once I had this support, I needed to go forward and do the necessary work to conquer my feelings of inadequacy. I did not need to rely continually on the instructor to "help" me.

Even today, sometimes I write something, lose a little confidence, and then need to ask someone for feedback. But after a short moment of dependency I am able to take my next step forward.

What did I do prior to receiving encouragement from my instructor? I inappropriately relied on my girlfriend. When I needed something written, I wanted her to do it for me, and I put pressure on her until she did it. If she hesitated, I became angry. After all, I reminded her, she claimed she loved me. Then she would give in and do my report or letter just to keep me happy. In doing this, we became co-dependent on each other in this area. I'm sure we were co-dependent in other areas also.

However, the more she helped, or rescued, me the more shame I felt and the more dependent on her I became. Since she had a need to keep me happy (her co-dependency), she continued to participate in this mutually shame-producing relationship.

Thus, a man who feels inadequate as the result of childhood abuse cannot expect or demand that his wife, children, or the rest of the world perform in certain ways to help him cover up and hide from his feelings of inadequacy. He must choose to face these feelings head-on. He needs the support of others, but only to face the truth of his own pain.

In the same way, a woman who was sexually abused cannot expect her husband to magically take away all her feelings of shame, loneliness, and broken trust just by the simple fact that he is married to her. At some point she will need to enter some form of therapy to heal these wounds. While she is going through the process of uncovering the ugliness of her past and the shame associated with such evil, her husband's love will be very important. But she cannot expect him to take out his magic eraser and make her past disappear.

PERSONAL RESPONSIBILITY

All of us have areas of our selfhoods that in the past were bruised and, consequently, shamed. We need outside sources of love to help heal these areas. Unfortunately, the more significant the violation, the more we may find ourselves at the mercy of others for emotional survival. But this dependency factor can be a huge trap for needy or deeply wounded individuals. It can set them up to be taken advantage of, to fall into poor relationships, to become co-dependent, and even to become victims of inappropriate types of therapy.

If you suffer from the shame of past violations and

you want to heal that shame, you face a set of delicate choices. To heal the shame you will need to trust in some outside source of love and affirmation, but you are responsible for choosing the right source. A part of choosing to heal this shame is discovering any destructive dependent relationships that are keeping you from healing this shame and then remove yourself from them.

The paradox of the dependency factor is that outside sources of love and affirmation are absolutely necessary in the healing process, but as an adult you cannot expect or demand affirmation from anyone. As a child you had a right to expect unconditional love and affirmation from your parents. But as an adult you do not have the right to demand that from your spouse, your children, your friends, your therapist, or whomever you need to heal your pain.

As scary as it may feel, to heal your shame you must pull back from your inappropriate sources of dependency to heal this shame and reestablish proper relationships. In the process of pulling back, you will find appropriate sources of support, and this will become the basis for the healing of your inner self.

CHAPTER FIVE

Healing Destructive Shame

No one walks through life without being emotionally wounded many times. These wounded parts are usually pushed down into the subconscious, especially when the self-esteem is not strong enough to directly face the violations.

Remember when George made me feel guilty for not voting? Even in that small incident, my mind needed to quickly rush in to protect my selfhood. It needed to do that because I had made myself vulnerable to George by responding to him honestly. He took my response and used it against me.

At the moment George violated me, my mind quickly came to my rescue and denied the violation. Not until a few minutes later, when I began to feel guilty, did I recognize the violation. My mind had to momentarily block out the incident. But, because I was emotionally strong enough, my self-esteem, or self-love, was sufficient to face the incident on my own. I had the strength to bring the truth of the incident to full consciousness and deal with it properly.

When children are wounded, however, they must bury their wounds, because they do not have sufficient inner strength and self-esteem to handle them. This is true for the big wounds, such as physical or sexual abuse, but even the smallest rejection from a parent can overwhelm a child. A parent's rejection hurts because a parent plays a powerful role in a child's life. During the early years of a child's life when a parent is the primary source of affirmation, trust, and safety, the parent's acceptance is vital to the child's emotional survival. Later the child's peers are the primary sources of affirmation, and the smallest rejection from an important peer can crush a child.

The dependency factor states that, as we go through life accumulating wounds, we subsequently become dependent on outside sources of love to heal our wounds. In a sense these wounds stay buried begging to be healed. They act as an inner driving force, crying out to be loved and affirmed.

A woman who was sexually abused as a child is wounded in the area of her sexuality. This part of her needs to be reaffirmed. She may take one of two courses of action attempting to heal and/or protect this wounded part of her sexual identity. She might block out or deny her need for sexual intimacy or she might become promiscuous in an indirect attempt to find loving affirmation for this wounded area.

Think again of my voting incident with George. You could challenge me that I didn't need an outside source of affirmation to heal the wound by saying, "You healed that on your own." But actually I didn't. Because my self-esteem was strong enough, I had the strength in my mind to defend myself against the violation. This enabled me to stop the violation and heal myself to some degree. However, to this day a part of me is still wounded. That part still needs George to tell me he is sorry he hurt me and to affirm me. It is a small part—so small that it does not significantly affect me. But it is still there.

We have all been wounded. Our minds push down these wounding events. Our wounded parts are the shamed areas of our selfhood. Eventually these parts resurface and need to be healed. Yet, because of broken trust, our minds will not allow these wounded parts to be directly known. Consequently, our wounds are known to us only indirectly as they cause addictions, compulsions, perfectionism, the need to control others, and other psychiatric disorders. Often we need professional therapists to help heal these wounded areas by establishing properly affirming therapeutic relationships where our wounded selves can emerge to begin the healing process.

By looking specifically at several forms of severely damaging abuse, such as verbal abuse, physical abuse, and sexual abuse, we can more clearly understand the healing process for the wounds these forms of abuse cause. We can also see more clearly how to heal wounds caused by other kinds of abuse as well.

VERBAL ABUSE

Several years ago, when Doug, a young man in his early thirties, began therapy, he was severely crippled with shame. Doug was one of the most gentle and honest men I had ever met, but throughout his life he had been criticized daily by his father who wanted him to be a professional athlete.

In the beginning we worked on the little issues— Doug's lack of self-confidence and the day-to-day events that caused him to feel false guilt. We worked on these issues by using the steps I discussed in Chapter Three. With great dedication and courage Doug made significant progress. But he was still filled with shame, mostly because his mind chose to avoid dealing with the deeper pain.

Eventually Doug began to open up and deal with the actual events that caused his destructive shame. For instance, on one occasion, when Doug was about twelve years old, his father attempted to instruct him on how to hit a baseball. When Doug did not perform with the skill his father expected, the father became infuriated and started deliberately throwing the ball at Doug's head, hitting him several times and finally knocking him to the ground. When Doug started to cry, his father walked to him, stood over him, and verbally abused him by calling him a sissy and a failure.

How did I help Doug heal this pain and corresponding shame? First, Doug had to be willing to share the event with me. We had already established an affirming relationship as we worked through other issues so that Doug did not fear revealing this event to me. Then, he had to let up some of the pain. As he did, he began to cry. Instead of verbally abusing him the way his father had, I let Doug know that his father's actions were wrong, and, perhaps more importantly, I reached over and gave Doug a hug. He felt my affirmation at the same time he was reliving the pain of his father's abuse.

In subsequent sessions we went more deeply into the pain of Doug's shame. As he got in touch with his felt shame, I directed him by saying something like, "Now take that shame and turn it into anger . . . Tell me what your anger wants to say . . . Say it out loud. Say, 'Dad, you hurt me. You hurt me deeply. You made me feel bad about myself, and I am angry at you for it.'"

Reliving the painful event and feeling the pain was an important step. Turning the pain into anger and expressing the anger was vital for Doug's healing. But, in order to release the shame, Doug needed an outside source of affirmation to truly heal. I encouraged him to look at me and ask, "Am I okay with you, Ty?" I responded that he was more than okay. He was a beautiful human being.

As the shame of these events began to gradually disappear, Doug's mind needed fewer and fewer thoughts of false guilt to keep the pain down. The more Doug felt loved and affirmed, the more his mind could think positively about himself and release his destructive shame.

The healing process included eight parts. Let's look at them one at a time and consider how Doug used them in his healing.

1. *A strong personal commitment to healing:* Doug was so filled with negative feelings, negative thoughts, and ways to sabotage himself that healing often seemed impossible to him. Starting on that road meant he would have to dig into all his pain. That meant he had to be committed to the healing process.

2. *Verbal or cognitive affirmation:* I needed to remind Doug many times of his potential, his good qualities, and his worth as a person. My verbal affirmation and the affirmation of others helped to replace his father's verbal disaffirmations.

3. *Cognitive restructuring:* Doug had so many ways of creating negative thoughts that I had to help him learn to think properly about himself. We used cognitive restructuring, or positive self-talk and positive thinking, to help him fight against his false guilt.

4. *Healing the emotional pain:* All the buried hurt had caused Doug to store up many tears. To

help him let up and release the pain, I needed to help him understand that he could cry. For the first time since he was a teenager, he allowed himself to shed tears caused by his emotional pain.

5. *Freedom to be angry:* Doug was a kind, gentle man, who rarely allowed himself to express anger. I needed to teach him how to appropriately feel and express his anger.

6. *Confronting the offender:* Doug's father had mellowed over the years and had become aware of his cruelty. Doug was able to sit down with him and talk. As they did, for the first time in his life, Doug felt his father's love. Unfortunately, such healing conditions with a parent are not always possible. When that is the case, writing the parent a letter that isn't mailed, visiting the parent's grave, or talking through the feelings with a therapist can help.

7. *Faith in God:* Doug was a deeply religious man. Knowing that God loved him and wanted him healthy helped him through some of his tougher moments.

8. *Proper dependency:* Establishing proper healing relationships was a major part of Doug's healing process. Because of his need for an ac-

cepting father figure, Doug had been a part of several inappropriate relationships with both men and women. For example, a businessman and a very self-centered minister had taken advantage of his over-dependence.

In therapy Doug began to establish with me a proper trusting and honest relationship. It was the first time in his life that he'd been involved in a healthy relationship. At the same time he was beginning a new relationship with a woman he had recently begun to date. She was in therapy with another therapist. They discussed with each other all their "old" ways of triggering people into unhealthy relationships and both grew tremendously during this time as they helped each other.

From this foundation of new, proper relationships, Doug slowly began to eliminate shame from his life, to feel more control over his mind's compulsive desire to produce false guilt, and to create proper, nondemanding, affirming relationships. As a result, a very desperate man took the responsibility to properly reach out in all areas of his life to heal himself.

We have all been verbally abused at different times in our lives. Right now I can think of several instances when I was verbally abused, especially a few painful ones with my peers at school. As I recall those times I can still feel some of the pain. It is still there inside me, but it is small—so small that it does not significantly affect my selfhood or my ability to love myself and enjoy life. Nevertheless, if I were to share these events in a group and recall the pain, or if I were to have a therapist help facilitate the painful feelings, most likely I would feel a healing.

I recommend you take a look at the verbal abuse in your life. How much is there and how are you still crippled by it? Do you cripple yourself with your own verbal abuse toward your selfhood? If you constantly put yourself down or think badly about yourself, that is a good indication that some kind of abuse took place that needs to be healed.

Don't let shame continue to rot your precious selfhood. Do whatever is necessary to begin the healing process.

PHYSICAL ABUSE

Extreme physical abuse is a special kind of abuse. For example, when a father hits a child, the child's trust is broken in a particular way.

A child needs to have his body physically protected by his father and naturally expects that protection. When his father hits him, he doesn't become ashamed of his personhood as much as he would if his father verbally abused him. Neither does he feel shame about his sexual body as he would if he were sexually abused. He becomes angry with his father and the physical abuse leaves the child with an intense rage. He will feel some shame that must be worked through. But he will have a strong component of rage toward his father which, if not properly dealt with, will most likely lead to destructive physical behavior toward others.

The problem is that the rage he feels toward his father is somewhat justified. Therefore, he feels justified in letting it up. Eventually he feels justified in venting his rage by physically abusing others. Yet after he abuses others, he feels intense shame for his actions.

A man who beats his wife or children, for example, feels justified at the time, but afterward he often feels great remorse. He may even make a commitment to never again duplicate such acts. But unless he does the necessary shame-anger work, he will be trapped forever by his rage and shame. His rage will continue to come up and be acted upon, followed by intense feelings of shame. This shame, which he brings on himself, further bruises the same spot that was wounded when he was physically abused, creating an even greater need to rage. Without proper healing, he may eventually feel the need to become destructive to himself or to push down all awareness of his shame, which increases his need to be abusive toward others.

If you were physically abused and are afraid of anger or have a tendency to explode in anger, working on your shame and anger will help heal and stabilize your out-of-control behavior. Cognitive work or trying to calm your mind down will only help some. The deep wounds left by the physical abuse must be dealt with directly.

SEXUAL ABUSE

Sexual abuse and sexual violations have a unique dependency factor that puts some boundaries on the healing process other kinds of abuse do not have. I can best explain this by using Doug's experience to demonstrate the differences.

Doug was verbally abused by his father, a man. I could help Doug facilitate the healing process by doing just the opposite of what his father had done by verbally affirming him. Doug also received verbal affirmation from his girlfriend and a support group. Eventually his father affirmed him, also. Doug's experience with me, his therapist, and the others was the kind of affirmation most people need in order to heal and eliminate overwhelming shame from their lives. But with the sexually abused, the needs for healing are different.

Once a person's sexuality is wounded, much of the shame cannot be healed until a proper sexual relationship is developed. This relationship must be trusting, honest, open, and intimate in order to overcome the depth of the violation that sexual abuse usually causes. Consequently, therapy has significant limitations that both the therapist and the client must observe.

With Doug I felt almost totally unrestricted in my freedom to affirm him verbally to undo the harm his father had caused. But with sexual abuse, the therapist—whether male or female—ultimately cannot undo the abuse the client suffered in the ways I could attempt to undo the harm Doug's father had done to him. Sexual abuse wounds the deepest, most intimate parts of the individual, and the therapist and anyone else who attempts to affirm the wounded person must be very careful not to violate his or her boundaries.

Tom came to me with a specific sexual problem. He'd been married a few months and had been unable to consummate the marriage. During foreplay he would feel an erection begin, but as soon as he became aware of it, it would quickly subside.

In therapy Tom revealed his mother had sexually abused him when he was a child. Often during times of abuse, he was chastised for not achieving an erection with his mother. When he couldn't "perform," his mother ridiculed him, calling him a failure and saying he would never be a real man. Consequently, as a sexual person, Tom had a deep, unconscious fear of failure.

Tom had blocked out many of the memories of his mother abusing him, pushing the pain way down, until he thought he was rid of it. When he met Susan, he believed they would have a satisfying marital relationship. She was loving and affirming—very different from his mother. However, when he and Susan tried to be intimate, his fear of failure would surface and Tom would feel paralyzed, questioning not only his sexuality, but his total worth as a person.

Susan was in therapy also with another therapist, working on the issues of shame resulting from her own abuse by her stepfather. Neither Susan's therapist nor I could affirm Susan or Tom in a way that would undo the harm they had suffered from their abusers, but we could help them work through their problems together and affirm each other. In other words, Tom and Susan were dependent on each other's help in the healing process. With Susan and Tom's permission, the other therapist and I consulted and developed a plan to help them create the trust they both needed to achieve a proper affirming sexual relationship. Today they have a beautiful marriage and two healthy children.

With Tom and Susan the dependency factor was solved in several different ways. First, each of them took the risk of sharing their abusive pasts with a therapist. Depending on therapy for the cognitive aspect only and some emotional release, they both worked through to clear understandings of their feelings associated with their abuses. They also took another healthy step when they allowed their therapists to work together.

The final and most important step occurred as they allowed their therapists to instruct them in taking the first steps in the sexual part of their relationship. Much hugging, kissing, and body massaging was freely exchanged as they learned to trust each other and eventually to achieve a proper relationship free of shame.

Without a doubt some of the most deeply embedded shame is caused by incest, sexual molestation, and rape. In these acts a very special inner part of an individual is violated, leaving the person feeling angry and dirty about his or her sexual identity.

In physical or verbal abuse a person can resist to some degree. But in sexual abuse, the victim's body is used by someone else against the victim. It is much harder for the victim to resist the abuse because many times the victim has a need to be touched. For example, a child may give over to abuse because he or she needs affirmation and physical contact.

The most important point to understand in the healing of sexual shame is the dependency factor. A part of the person's sexuality has been taken away—murdered, so to speak. That part can be only partially healed through cognitive or talk therapy. A part of the person's body will always cry out for a physical or sexual healing until the dependency factor has been properly affirmed and satisfied.

In other words, if you were sexually abused, a part of your body may feel a strong need to be sexually satisfied, not just because of your present sexual desires, but also because of your body's need to heal those past wounds. This unconscious desire will cause you either to give yourself away at times when you don't want to or to fear sexual involvement even in marriage.

Thus the abused person must take full charge of this dependency factor if he or she wants to ever heal these wounds properly. It is not wrong to desire or need the physical part of the healing. Think about how much hugging takes place at a funeral where people are comforting each other to replace the felt physical loss of their loved one.

The physical part of the healing is not wrong. However, refraining from sex will not heal; neither will indiscriminate sexual contact. Therefore, where wounds of sexual abuse are present, I suggest that you find a competent therapist trained to treat victims of sexual abuse, talk through the abuse, begin letting the painful feelings up, and begin learning how to set proper boundaries.

When you feel you have moved as far as possible in the healing process, then begin a relationship if you are not currently in one. When you are comfortable share a part of the abuse with your partner. See how he or she reacts to the wounds to your sexual identity and the attempts you are making to become healed. Take this information back to your therapist. I would even suggest talking through some of the abuse with your partner together with the therapist if the relationship continues to grow.

When you have been violated, the violation robs you of your ability to love yourself in that area. You are hungry to be loved in this one area and thus become dependent on others. The woundedness results in feelings of abandonment, loneliness, and jealousy that cause you to fall prey to inappropriate relationships. Consequently, those who have been sexually abused often suffer further sexual abuse in their adult relationships.

The shame of past sexual abuse can take several forms in an adult. Promiscuity and choosing to have sex to avoid rejection are only two. The person who fears relationships and consequently avoids marriage is suffering a self-inflicted form of sexual abuse as well. The sexual part of his or her identity desires and cries out to be loved, healed, and fulfilled. In denying him or herself, the individual pushes down the shame of past events and continues the cycle of shame and denial.

LIFTING FALSE GUILT TO HEAL THE SHAME

A thirty-five-year-old woman entered therapy to work on issues of depression, anxiety, and an eating disorder. In order to uncover the buried shame and heal the pain of the violations that caused it, in each session she had to lift a little of the false guilt, feel some of the shame, battle it with her anger and affirmation, feel the hurt, and finally experience some healing. Her mind had buried her shame because the pain of it was too great for her to handle, and she had created false guilt as a tool to bury the shame more deeply and attempt to control it. Her false guilt came originally from her parents as they severely abused her, but she created additional false guilt to push down the overwhelming shame of their abuses.

I'm using this woman's case history to demonstrate the process of healing shame and to show more clearly what happens when an individual lifts the protective coating of false guilt and uncovers buried shame. Allowing shame to surface does involve a risk.

An individual, whether child or adult, is damaged most when his or her ability to feel self-love is destroyed.

Helping the individual heal his or her pain and rebuild self-esteem is a delicate process. The process must take place in a safe environment where the individual can experience affirmation and loving support when he or she confronts denial and false guilt, relives the violations, and feels the pain of them without the risk of further damage.

This woman—we'll call her Rose—was sexually abused by both her parents from the time she was five years old until she was nine. Each parent knew the other was abusing Rose and each used this "secret" to abuse her further, while blaming her for being sexually involved with the other. Not only did Rose feel dirty and shamed for the abuses, her parents created a tremendous amount of false guilt when they told her she was to blame for their abuse. Rose added additional false guilt to cover and tolerate her pain, continually telling herself, "I am bad." But she could not keep the pain completely hidden. Something would touch her wounded part and the shame would begin to surface. Rose would feel a compulsion to scratch and cut herself. She thought of the scratches and cuts as punishment she deserved, and the self-mutilation gave her a sense of forgiveness that empowered her to push the shame back down to keep it from destroying her. However, because Rose wasn't guilty of any wrongdoing, the amends she tried to make (by punishing herself) did not promote healing of her selfhood. The self-mutilation merely reburied her pain until the next time it was stirred up.

Rose's case is an extreme one and helping her required a highly skilled therapist. But the process Rose needed for her healing was similar to the process anyone needs to heal deeply embedded shame. Her therapy sessions show the pattern.

Rose began to talk about a part of her past. After a few moments, the therapist interrupted, asking Rose what she was feeling. Rose usually replied, "I feel bad."

The therapist took a moment to affirm Rose by telling her *she* was not bad, but what *her parents* did to her was bad. Then the therapist began to deal with the shame by reminding Rose, "The only way to work through the shame is to use the power of your anger." The therapist gave Rose a soft rubber bat and asked, "What does your anger want to say?" Typically Rose replied, "It's not my fault. It's not my fault!"

When the violations took place, Rose's mind needed to wall off the pain to keep the shame from destroying her selfhood. Hearing the therapist affirm that she wasn't bad helped Rose to think correctly and dissolve her defense mechanism of false guilt. Then Rose could say aloud that she had not been responsible for her violations and begin feeling the anger the abuse had caused. But as the defense mechanism of false guilt was lifted, there was nothing left to hold down the shame. At this point the shame would begin to overwhelm her, compelling her to scratch at her body, at times ripping open her skin. With the false guilt momentarily removed, Rose needed to punish herself in attempts to regain control of the shame.

At this point the therapist had to work hard and fast to help Rose use her anger to fight the shame. When Rose was a child she had no one to help or affirm her and she didn't have the strength necessary to fight either the violations or the shame they caused. As an adult, she had to take courage and conquer the shame. But by holding onto her denial and false guilt, telling herself she was bad and needed to be punished, Rose could keep her mind away from the shame and push it back down.

As Rose began to mutilate her body, the therapist caught Rose's hands and said, "I will not let you hurt yourself. Use your anger. Pick up the bat and use the power of your anger to overcome the shame."

INCREASED DEPTH OF REPRESSED FEELINGS	
Depression, anxiety, eating disorders, etc.
False guilt
Shame
Anger
Pain of the violation (tears)
Inner peace, joy, and love

Rose grabbed the bat and began hitting a pillow. She did not need to become excessively angry, but she did need to get in touch with her anger, verbalize it, and use it to dissolve her shame. When she finished, she usually felt some tears. Allowing herself to cry finally exposed the wound to be truly healed. Over a period of time, a deep inner joy about her life—an emotion she had not experienced before she began the healing process—began replacing the memories of the abuse and the shame.

The illustration on page 80 illustrates the levels of feeling Rose walked through each time she worked on her negative self-image and destructive behavior.

RE-LOVING

Rose was caught in a trap. Her mind needed to keep the guilt and shame buried to keep the pain away. That meant her mind had to hold onto her negative self-image and perpetuate her destructive behavior. Keeping the guilt and shame buried and the pain under control required additional false guilt which added to her negative self-image and made her behavior even more destructive.

She had to learn how to re-love herself so that she could be independent of her past wounds and think positively about herself. Eventually she could make proper choices for herself and correctly reach out for affirmation.

Healing your self-esteem of shame is hard work. It is not as easy as reading a few books, listening to a few tapes, and doing a little guided imagery. Shame work often requires a tremendous amount of skill and patience on the part of the therapist or support person. It also requires the individual's determination to look at and heal the pain behind the shame and learn to re-love himself.

Most individuals will not feel destructive shame to the degree that Rose felt it. But the healing process is much the same. The person must get below the surface symptoms and the false guilt to expose the shame. Only when the violation is healed will true inner peace or self-love be possible.

CHAPTER SIX

The Complex Nature of Guilt

Life has a way of compounding situations, and guilt is no exception. For the Christian, guilt can often be a serious problem when actually religious beliefs should diminish problems with guilt. Sometimes we encounter events that trigger enormous amounts of guilt that the precipitating events don't warrant. At other times we suffer lingering guilt—paralyzing, ongoing responses to events or situations from the past that we cannot change or alleviate. Other situations contain components of both true guilt and false guilt. Defining personal responsibility and knowing where to seek help seem difficult.

The complexity of these guilt-producing situations requires some careful thought to differentiate between true guilt and false guilt and know when and how to make amends and eliminate these emotions from our lives.

THE RELIGIOUS WOUND

Guilt and anger are often associated with our religious beliefs, but from a Christian, biblical perspective, guilt should not be a problem for a believer. The Bible teaches that God created us in an act of love, that He loves each of us personally, and that He forgives us when we stumble or fall. Still often a Christian feels great guilt and anger, much of these emotions inappropriate and unnecessary.

We can be wounded spiritually just as we can be wounded in other aspects of our lives. When we disobey God, we should feel guilt and a desire to confess and ask forgiveness. This true guilt awakens our minds so we can experience God's love and come back to a state of joy about ourselves, our spirituality, and our relationship with Him.

We can come to a point, however, of not being able to receive God's love because we have violated His law or someone has violated our spirituality. Our wrong behaviors produce true guilt and some shame, but violations of our spirituality produce false guilt and destructive shame.

The Bible deals with true guilt, the result of humankind's sinful, rebellious nature. As with all other forms of true guilt, resolving and eliminating sin is quite simple. We must repent and ask God's forgiveness. A basic foundation of Christianity is that Jesus Christ died on the Cross to make it possible for our sins to be forgiven. When we acknowledge the deity of Jesus Christ and accept Him as our Lord and Savior, we have the assurance of God's love and His forgiveness.

We know from this that God uses our true guilt, not to punish us, but to bring us back into proper relationship with Him and others. Thus, if we disobey God, we shouldn't feel smashed or torn apart by guilt. We should let Him love and affirm us and help us live obediently.

We feel false religious guilt when someone attacks the innocence of our spirituality. Rather than focusing on our irresponsible or sinful behavior, some try to use God against us by shaming us.

A parent can destroy the love potential of a child by attacking the child's self-worth and attempting to make the child feel bad about who he is as a person. (Remember, shame has more to do with a person's selfhood, whereas guilt has more to do with a person's behavior.) Those who attack our spirituality attack in the same way—they destroy our spiritual self-worth.

Religious shame begins with false guilt by damaging an individual's spirituality. One person makes another feel bad or worthless before God by telling him that unless he is a certain way, God will not love him. Some go one step further and attempt to control an individual by never letting him or her feel quite okay before God. These people make sure an element of guilt is always in the individual's mind interfering with God's love. Some, those whose own spirituality is wounded, seem even to feel a need to purposely wound or abuse the spirituality of others.

They tell an individual that God hates him or wants to punish him. They may even say that the wounds the individual has from other sources were inflicted as God's punishment. Their worst violation may be in telling an individual that he cannot possibly be good enough to be worthy of God's love and must constantly deny himself in order to try to make amends.

This kind of attack leaves a person with feelings of hurt, guilt, and anger toward God. The guilt-ridden person is not able to think about God without feeling shame or thinking guilt-producing thoughts. The person whose spirituality has been wounded in this way often becomes a compulsive church worker as a self-sacrifice to be good enough to be loved. Or he may reject God and live constantly in fear of God and life in general. He or she may become extremely angry with God or subconsciously need to come to the intellectual conclusion that God does not exist in order to push down these feelings. Trying to prove that God does not exist is often an attempt to defeat God or punish Him. Most likely what this person feels is a need to punish the people who hurt him.

Spiritual wounds are healed the same way other wounds are healed, but first, the wounded person needs to have a correct understanding of God. It is important that he or she realize there is nothing we can do to lose God's love. He does not hate us. Each of us is infinitely valuable to Him. He only wants us to repent of our disobedient behavior so that love and joy can flow. If we are willing to come before God on this basis, then we can release our guilt. If any feelings of guilt remain, they are false guilt and destructive shame and come from feelings of badness we have about ourselves.

These feelings do not come from God. Either we imposed them on ourselves, or they came from others who violated our spiritual innocence. To heal these feelings, we must let up the pain of the feelings (the hurt, loneliness, guilt, and anger) and interface it with God's unconditional love.

Part of the healing can be accomplished by getting involved with a church that is filled with acceptance rather than one that teaches guilt and anger. The members of such a church desire to follow God's laws and are willing to repent when a law is broken. This church body freely feels and acknowledges that God loves each one of us unconditionally, and it is based on the foundational principles of God's eternal grace.

If you are aware of specific anger, guilt, or feelings of worthlessness associated with God or the church, you may need to sit down with a counselor or minister and talk through these feelings, as well as the events in your past that caused them. You may even need to cry, become angry, and be held and prayed for.

To help you better understand guilt and your relationship to God, it will be helpful to be clear about how God intervenes in each one of the different kinds of guilt and shame. Of the four different kinds of guilt and shame, God directly helps us with only one—*true guilt*. With the others, we need to help ourselves, and sometimes each other, while asking Him to give us insight, courage, and the ability to forgive others when we need to.

True guilt is the only guilt that God directly helps us with because His acceptance and forgiveness are what ultimately set us free. We purposely go against a part of His creation and His authority when we break one of God's laws. That is a spiritual issue between the individual and God. Resolving it and healing the guilt requires the individual to repent. Then God will forgive and help correct wrong behavior. Since God is more than willing to forgive each one of us, it is up to the individual to repent.

With *false guilt* there was no wrongful act. Asking God to forgive means that the individual imposes on himself or allows someone else to impose on him the assumption that he actually did something wrong when he didn't. Therefore, there is nothing for God to forgive, and begging Him to forgive doesn't relieve us of our false guilt. We must do the work on this one.

A very small amount of *constructive shame* is a good shame; so there is no need to remove it or ask God to forgive it.

Destructive shame gets a little tricky. God helps with our deep shame because He loves us wholly—even where we are wounded. We suffer destructive shame because someone violated us, making a part of us unlovable. We can take the wounds to God and ask Him to heal us, but we need other people to help heal our shame. To be whole, to restore self-esteem, we must interact with other people. That is the way God made us.

Picture a little boy who was teased and beaten up at school coming home to seek comfort from his mother. If his mother simply tells him, "Go to your room, pray, feel God's love, and you will be okay," there would be little real healing. The little boy needs his mother's arms around him. He needs to hear her words of comfort and affirmation. God doesn't take away destructive shame directly because we need to be accountable to each other and to be a part of each other's healing.

When George criticized me unjustly for not voting, he created some false guilt in me. When I finally recognized it, I had no trouble reversing the process from guilt to a little anger. George also wounded part of my selfhood. It is a very small part, but when I focus on it, I can still feel the wound and my need for him to help in the healing. My innocence was hurt by a person, so I need a person (either George or someone else) in the healing process. The assurance of God's love helps me, but I need to feel the warmth of another human being.

Often we see a person, a drug addict, for example, "come to the Lord" and almost overnight become compulsive about or addicted to his religious beliefs. Partly he feels great joy because his true guilt has been forgiven. Partly his compulsive behavior is an attempt to use his religion to keep away from the deeper shame that can only be healed through hard therapeutic work.

If you identify with this section, if you are a person who has been spiritually wounded or who does not feel deeply healed by your faith, I strongly encourage you to seek a proper solution. Why carry unhealed guilt, anger, and fear of God throughout your life? That hurts you and keeps you from enjoying the love God has for you. The ones who profit from your wounds are the ones who hurt you, while you remain a victim and rob yourself of joy in one of the most important areas of your life. That certainly is not what God wants for you. It shouldn't be what you want, either.

GHOSTS FROM THE PAST

Often we encounter situations that cause us to be suddenly overwhelmed with enormous amounts of guilt. This guilt can cripple us instantly, sending us into a tailspin. The precipitating event might not be responsible for all the guilt. It's possible that the event may have released or penetrated a pocket of guilt locked up from the past. A few years ago I witnessed a tragic car accident that caused this kind of guilt to be released.

A car was turning left when the two women in it were suddenly blinded by the sun. At the same moment an elderly man stepped into the intersection and began crossing the street. The car hit him hard enough to kill him instantly. It was an unfortunate accident and all parties were innocent of wrongdoing as well as irresponsible behavior.

About thirty minutes later I noticed that the two women were sitting on the curb, and one of them was sobbing uncontrollably. I walked over to ask if I could help, and I was surprised to learn that Pam, the passenger, not Lisa, the driver, was the one who was crying and suffering overwhelming guilt. She blamed herself for somehow not preventing the accident. I talked with them for a while and when I left, I asked for their phone numbers and I called them later to check on them.

That evening Lisa was feeling a lot of guilt, yet she knew she was innocent of any wrongdoing. Her self-esteem was intact enough that she could move away from her guilt-producing thoughts and stay with the pain of the situation. As she dwelled on the accident, she knew her mind was taking the pain and turning it to guilt to try to eliminate the pain of the event. But since she knew it was not her fault and she had the strength to force her mind back to the pain, she could let her pain up to heal this wound. But Pam's response was different.

Pam had grown up with a controlling, perfectionist, guilt-ridden mother, and she had learned the habit of blaming herself for events outside her control. So when the accident happened, Pam's self-esteem was not strong enough to hold in place all the unhealed shame she had been pushing down since her childhood. The accident caused the pain of these unhealed wounds to suddenly come up, and her mind went crazy with guilt.

Pam's mind created false guilt for the same reason that Lisa's did, but it was the shame of her past that was driving Pam's mind close to an emotional breakdown. When I learned Pam had been in therapy before, I recommended she go back to her therapist and do some more work.

The unhealed guilt and/or shame of a person's past can magnify everyday events. As healthy adults, we should be able to handle even catastrophic events, such as the death of a loved one, or war, or a tragic car accident.

I don't mean to imply that we should not be affected by catastrophes. A healthy person should be. But like Lisa, if we are emotionally healthy, we can face such events because we are only dealing with the present event and can reach out for appropriate help.

Hidden guilt and shame from the past will force us to overcompensate, lose control, become fearful, and experience panic attacks and other severe psychological symptoms. Past events make us crazy because of their magnitude and because we don't know the source of the pain or guilt. We have the tendency to attach this past pain to the current event.

If an event makes you become unstable and present support doesn't bring about a healing, then look for past wounded, unhealed parts of your selfhood.

LINGERING GUILT

Sometimes we do things that cause others harm, perhaps even permanent harm. Being an alcoholic, putting a family through bankruptcy, having a car accident in which someone is injured, or realizing that we were not the best parents we could have been are just some situations that can cause guilt to linger indefinitely.

Tina always made her children wear seatbelts. *Always*—except one time. The day she made an exception to her rule, she was in a hurry. It was only a short distance home and her daughter was having trouble fastening the seatbelt. Tina didn't take the time to help her daughter with it. She said, "This time we won't worry about it." In only a few minutes, another car hit them head-on. Tina's daughter was seriously injured, and her injuries resulted in almost complete paralysis.

Robert is a high-level executive who lost his job because his drinking problem caused him to be absent from work too often. His family suffered through the humiliation of losing their home when he couldn't find another job.

Morgan, who said, "I need money to make money," risked his children's college fund on an investment that went sour. Then he "borrowed" from his company's account to cover the loss.

These situations are not easy to deal with. The guilt and shame are likely to be overwhelming and to linger on and on. For the rest of her life, every time Tina looks at her daughter she will be reminded that her momentary negligence may have contributed significantly to her daughter's permanent disability. Robert's shame over the effect his drinking had on his family, as well as his career, may cause him to try to hide from it by drinking more. And Morgan, who can never erase the memory of being arrested and put on trial, must face the fact that his greed affected not only his children's future, but the other employees of his company as well.

For any of these people, holding on to the guilt and shame does no one any good. In fact, it could cause additional harm to those who have already been harmed. The first step toward healing is to go to the ones who were harmed, confess the wrongdoing, and ask forgiveness. Then whatever behavior needs to be changed must be changed.

Perhaps Tina's habit of trying to squeeze too many activities into her day and consequently always being a little late contributed to her decision to not take the few seconds that fastening her daughter's seatbelt would have required. Tina may need to work on being more realistic about what she can accomplish in a given period of time.

Robert will need to face his alcoholism and stop his substance abuse. He will likely need professional help and may need to enter a treatment program. Typically substance abusers have great denial systems, partly to bury the guilt. Robert will have to work through his denial and acknowledge that abusing alcohol is irresponsible behavior and that the guilt he feels is true guilt. He won't be able to begin eliminating his guilt until he has stopped his addiction.

Morgan may try to convince himself that serving a prison sentence paid his "debt" and taught him "a lesson," but he also will need to work hard on the issues that caused him to think, even momentarily, that it would be all right to steal.

Real forgiveness and release of guilt do not take place until we have recognized and changed the behaviors that caused us to act wrongfully. We must be willing to look inside ourselves and find the behaviors that need to be changed and then do the work necessary to try to change them. It is hard for those we've harmed to forgive us if we are still behaving irresponsibly.

The next step toward healing is to make amends where possible. This is an important step and it must be done carefully, keeping in mind what it means to "make amends." It means "to correct." In a sense it means "to restore."

Morgan might feel that once he had served his prison sentence, he had made amends. But sending him to prison was society's way of punishing him for breaking a law, and it didn't restore the money he stole. For Morgan, making amends starts with trying to pay back the money.

In Tina's case, however, there is nothing she can do to restore her daughter's body. She can give her daughter plenty of love and provide her with the best medical care and therapy possible. But if Tina continually tries to make amends by giving up her own life to become a slave to her daughter's needs, she will do further harm to them both. Tina will always need to fight against her guilt, but she must realize that it is false guilt. Her mind creates it to try to deal with the daily pain of her daughter's paralysis.

Robert's need to make amends may be the easiest to satisfy and, at the same time, the most difficult. He can't make up to his family for the pain and harm his years of drinking caused them. He can only try to change his behavior and to rebuild their trust.

These three steps—seek forgiveness, change wrong

or irresponsible behavior, and make amends where possible—are the way to eliminate guilt and heal the pain. But they aren't all the steps needed. There's one final step, and it is the most important one. It can't be taken usually until the first three are finished, and for most people it is the most difficult step. You take the final step when you forgive yourself.

A passage in the Bible says, "As far as the east is from the west, so far has He removed our transgressions from us" (Ps. 103:12). It means that God knows our hearts and with His love and forgiveness separates our sins from us as though they'd never happened. He wants us to release them, too. That is the final step.

FINDING THE RIGHT HELP

Many situations contain components of both true and false guilt, and this causes tremendous confusion. The confusion can lead to an inability to seek the right kind of help. Consequently a religious person with a particular problem often doesn't know when to seek God through prayer or a minister and when to seek psychotherapy.

Theoretically, knowing where to find help is simple. True guilt is a spiritual problem because it involves morals, the evil side of man, God's love, and our rebellious natures toward God. False guilt is a psychological problem caused by the mind creating the emotion of false guilt primarily to deal with emotional pain. In other words, true or spiritual guilt is the result of our rebellious, defiant natures acting intentionally. False or psychological guilt is the result of others hurting us or our bringing pain to the lives of others *without* any intention to do them harm. True guilt must be dealt with by spiritual principles, such as confessing and asking to be forgiven. False guilt must be dealt with by psychological principles of healing.

If a religious couple is in an abusive, seemingly impossible-to-live-with marriage, what should they do? Should they divorce? If they divorce, will their guilt be true or false guilt? Specifically should they counsel with their pastor about spiritual issues or consult a psychologist about destructive communication patterns in their marriage?

If one or both parties grew up in abusive or dysfunctional families and married before they properly healed the wounds of their childhoods, producing a healthy marriage would be almost impossible. Elaine's story demonstrates the difficulty and the need to seek the right kind of help.

Elaine grew up in a very abusive home. Her father often came home drunk and beat up her mother and older brother. Because her mother was equally emotionally handicapped, Elaine took on the responsibility of holding the family together. During her high school years, her father began to hit her younger brother, too. Elaine felt extremely responsible for this brother and her father's beating him added to Elaine's sense of responsibility as well as the stress of her home life. Consequently, she began to have severe panic attacks.

After graduating from high school, Elaine's panic attacks were so severe and her need to escape the pain of her home was so great, she ran away. Shortly afterward she married.

In her new situation the panic attacks diminished and Elaine did fairly well emotionally until her first child was born. Her husband was often away on business, and she was alone with her baby and completely responsible for the child's welfare. Almost immediately she began to have panic attacks again, and she feared that her attacks would become so severe she would be unable to take care of her child. She discovered that a little alcohol helped lessen the severity of the attacks. Then after her second child was born and her feelings of panic increased, she discovered that a little more alcohol diminished the panic even more.

Soon Elaine was an alcoholic. Eventually she lost her marriage and both her children. She came to therapy filled with guilt and shame about her divorce and losing her children. She blamed herself for her drinking and for all that had happened to her.

Elaine's case history is an extreme example of a situation that contains both true and false guilt. But the majority of her guilt was false. She did not run away from home or begin drinking because she intentionally wanted to hurt anyone or to defy God. Elaine did what she did because that was the only way she knew to survive. Her guilt came from the pain of having to do what she did. She had to work through the wounds of her childhood, for which she wasn't responsible, before she could deal with any spiritual issues. Today Elaine is completely sober and has her children back. She is one of the best mothers I know.

I did not grow up in a highly dysfunctional family, so I did not enter marriage with significant unhealed wounds from my childhood. And both my wife and I were spiritually committed to our marriage. We should have been successful in producing a healthy marriage. However, at the age of twenty-five I felt extremely trapped. I thought I had to divorce or go crazy. We struggled for several years, trying to do everything we knew to save the marriage, but it seemed our only recourse was divorce. We did not seek counseling. At that time it wasn't as socially acceptable.

Now, twenty-four years later, I know the problem was our mutual lack of emotional maturity and our inability to communicate. Those were not spiritual issues. We couldn't pray them away or confess them. We needed help from a professional who was an expert in marriage and family relationships, just as Elaine needed a good therapist or psychologist to help her heal her childhood wounds.

Marriages do fail and not all the failures result from a lack of spiritual commitment. Often dysfunctional childhoods and/or emotional immaturity are the cause. We must be careful where we place the blame and we need to be willing to seek the correct kind of help.

We should not feel guilt or responsibility for our dysfunctional pasts or the psychological pain we suffer in the present. The fact that problems exist may not be an individual's fault, but he or she is responsible for seeking proper help. We are also responsible for our behavior today, regardless of our past histories.

Some people hesitate to seek counseling. They may need to question their degree of irresponsibility. By failing to work with a therapist on whatever issues they have, whether a substance abuse problem or something else, they may be refusing to acknowledge the problem. In such cases there is an element of true guilt.

Unless both parties in a marriage work hard to change, the marriage may be doomed. But if a couple goes to a trained counselor and says sincerely, "We both have dysfunctional areas of our lives; please help us," there is little doubt in my mind that most troubled marriages could be saved.

One problem I see frequently is that people seldom come into counseling and say, "My marriage is in trouble, and my spouse is unhappy. Show me what I need to change about myself and teach me how to do it." Instead, they come in hoping to change their spouses. Similarly, parents rarely come in with the attitude of wanting to be better parents by looking at their own behavior or issues. They hope the counselor will magically change their children. When parents do this, they are asking the child to take more of an adult role than they are taking.

Frank came to me a few years ago. He had recently started molesting his daughter. He said that often he felt an uncontrollable urge to sneak into his daughter's room and touch her. But if he did, within minutes he was overwhelmed with guilt and shame. Consequently, he would spend hours praying to God for help until he thought the urge was gone. A couple of weeks later he would feel the urge again, and the cycle would be repeated. Frank was a deeply religious man and an elder at his church, but he was very disturbed because the more he prayed, the less praying helped him. He felt his belief in God wasn't working.

Fortunately, Frank acted quite responsibly. He tried to stop the urge to molest his daughter twice on his own by being strong, focusing his mind on other things, and praying. The third time he knew he needed to seek professional help, and he came running in for therapy.

Frank was highly motivated and worked hard, and it didn't take long to figure out the problem. Frank had grown up with a very powerful, dominating mother and married a woman much like her. Consequently, he had felt powerless around women all his life. On a subconscious level, however, he wanted and needed to feel powerful around women. Frank's mind kept this desire locked away because he was unable to be consciously aware of it while he continued being dominated by women—a situation he thought he was powerless to change.

The more Frank's wife controlled him (including sexually) and the more his daughter grew up naturally wanting to please him, the more this subconscious need began to seek an outlet. The desire to sexually domi-

nate his daughter was his mind's attempt to find affirmation and relieve the pain of his inability to stand up
to his wife and mother.

When Frank's mind snapped back to reality, a flood
of guilt and shame would wash over him and make him
feel even smaller. This subconscious, wounded part had
only one way to affirm itself, and that was to molest his
daughter. Since the real problem had not been solved,
the need to molest her soon resurfaced.

This is basically the same process that results in
most, if not all, addictive and compulsive disorders.
Some wounded part of an individual surfaces subconsciously and attempts to affirm itself indirectly through
the addiction or compulsion.

What part of Frank's guilt was true guilt and what
part was false guilt? Or what part was he personally
responsible for?

He wasn't guilty or responsible for his sexual urge
toward his daughter. That was caused by wounds from
his dominating mother and his dysfunctional past. But
he was responsible for the acts he committed against his
daughter, because he knew that was wrong.

Ideally, Frank should feel just a little shame for his
inappropriate desires. But he should not condemn himself for the fact that he had them. He wasn't responsible
for these urges because they resulted from an inner
wounded part which was put there by his mother and
reinforced by his wife. Frank was responsible for allowing the thoughts to control him and grow, actually
abusing his daughter, and not working on his relation-

ships with his wife and mother. He was also responsible for not seeking help initially.

So many people who have problems, such as substance abuse, abnormal sexual behavior, and so forth, feel so much shame and guilt they avoid getting help. Yet by not seeking help, the false guilt and buried shame carry over into true guilt as they commit wrongful acts against themselves and others. Mixing these two kinds of guilt together only brings more confusion, further preventing the person seeking proper help.

To help Frank, we dealt with the issues of his past. I helped him establish a more open and honest relationship with his wife. In essence I taught him how to stand up to her and to his mother. Frank's mother continued to be a problem but his wife cooperated quite well. She actually preferred a husband with the strength to be himself. This part of Frank's selfhood healed and the urge to molest his daughter disappeared.

In the past the religious community was very much opposed to individuals seeking psychological help. Most Christians believed that all problems—no matter what the cause—could be dealt with spiritually. Over time, however, most denominations have come to agree that proper psychological help is not only valuable, but indispensable. Part of this new confidence is the result of advancements in psychotherapy. Yet still there are churches and ministers who preach that all a hurting individual needs to do is pray and have faith.

God wants us to pray to Him and be obedient, but He also wants us to take advantage of modern medical and psychological knowledge. Childhood issues, such as broken trust and lack of love and safety, are psychological issues; they must be dealt with from a psychological perspective.

If you need professional help, take time in choosing a proper therapist and/or clergyman. But most importantly, don't deny yourself help.

CHAPTER SEVEN

Searching for Your True Self

Throughout this book, I have stated several times that true guilt and constructive shame are both beneficial and fundamental to the growth of an individual's self. I've also tried to show you that false guilt and destructive shame are the elements that destroy a person's selfhood and identity. In this final chapter I want to leave you with the clearest possible understanding of how false guilt and destructive shame can destroy you and cause you to be confused about your identity.

In the early '70s, I worked as an outreach youth minister in the inner city of Los Angeles. As you might expect, the ministry ran on a shoestring. I purchased a house to use in the ministry and, in an attempt to stretch the money as far as possible and make the ministry work, I lived there practically in poverty. Eventually the ministry ran out of money and had to be closed. When I sold the house, I made a small profit.

At that time, many Christians were somewhat confused about wealth and whether it was spiritually appropriate for believers to spend money on themselves for more than the bare necessities of life. Some believed that anything beyond the basic essentials should be given away.

I wasn't especially confused about that issue, but I had struggled with my identity. Living and working in a culture that was different from the one I'd grown up in had caused me to question some of my values. Therefore, even as I felt it was appropriate to reward myself by buying a new car with the profit from the house, I was vulnerable to what others felt was right for me.

The car I bought was a BMW 2002. In 1975 it cost an amazingly low (compared to what such a car costs today) $7,400.

Soon after, I was asked to help run a youth camp in Colorado for a month. I packed my bags and jumped in my new car and thoroughly enjoyed driving it to the camp. The car caused quite a stir among the camp counselors and other staff, and in a few days I had been teased in just about every way possible. Most of the comments were kindly humorous, but in some of the joking I sensed sarcasm. A few people were critical of my having a new BMW, and they let me know indirectly with their teasing.

I felt okay with the way I had used the money, but the criticism began to wear on me, and I began to question my decision. I used a lot of energy rethinking it and wondering if I had done the right thing. Before long my self-esteem began to weaken. Then subconsciously I began to look for approval. As the teasing continued, I doubted myself more. As I doubted myself more, I became more dependent on outside authorities to determine what was right for me. As this spiral continued, I began to feel shame, and my mind wanted to turn it to false guilt. With each passing day, I felt a vagueness in my ability to know what was right for me. I was losing sight of who I was, what I wanted, and what was meaningful for me.

The point of telling this story is that it demonstrates the basic elements of false guilt and destructive shame. Some of the camp staff believed I shouldn't have a nice, new car. Those people thought I should have bought a cheap, used car, if I had to have one, and given the rest of the money away. They thought that was what they would have done if they had been me, and they wanted to impose their values on me. They did that by shaming my choice.

But I hadn't done anything wrong. I didn't steal the money. I didn't have a wife and children who would go hungry or lose their home because I had spent some money buying a new car. I hadn't harmed anyone, and I hadn't put myself in danger. I had made a healthy choice and it was my choice to make. Making it was a part of my freedom and personal authority to have my identity and develop self-esteem. I felt okay with my decision, but my critics were making me feel bad about myself. They were violating my innocence and trapping me with false guilt. To a degree I became a prisoner of the shame and somewhat dependent on the opinions of outside sources in order to feel okay. I was at risk to feel that I couldn't properly make decisions about myself and that I needed others to make my choices for me.

To be okay with ourselves, we must each have the strength to focus on ourselves and determine who we are and what is best for us. We do that by making our own mistakes, learning from our mistakes, using the learning in our growth toward maturity, and through trial and error, learning to properly focus on our own lives.

My sense of self was fairly strong and I was able to withstand the attacks. Even though I wavered a little, I never came close to seriously doubting myself. More importantly, at no time was I on the verge of rushing out to sell my car and then give the money away simply because my critics thought I should. If, on my own, without outside interference, I had decided I would rather have a less expensive car and give the rest of the money to the poor, that would have been a healthy decision, just as the decision to buy the car was a healthy one.

However, if I decided to sell the car only because my critics said I should—by calling me extravagant, saying I was a show-off, and worst of all, trying to label my car purchase a sin of pride—they would have been in control of me. They would have had their hands on the lens of my life, and I would be dependent on them to do the focusing. Later there would have been someone else who would want to impose his or her values on me and tell me what to do. Then someone else and someone else. Each time I would be less able to make my own decision and my self-esteem would diminish further, until I would be unable to think for myself.

This is what happens with children whose parents make too many choices for them, even if the choices are correct. The joy and excitement of learning to be independent people, of knowing how to decide "this is what is right for me," and even how to say, "I made a mistake," are gradually taken away from those who are prevented from making their own choices. The only healthy choices for any of us are those we freely make for ourselves. Even if some of our choices are the wrong ones, they are a part of our growth toward maturity and healthy self-esteem.

After about ten days at camp, Winston, one of the camp leaders, called me aside. He put his arm around my shoulders and said, "Don't let them get you down. Feel okay about your car."

Winston's simple statement had an astonishing effect on me. We all respected him. He had a strong, dominating presence. Most of his life he'd lived and worked in the ghettos of Pittsburgh. I thought that if anyone had a perspective on the proper relation of material possessions with the Christian life, it was Winston. I believed that, of all the people at camp, if anyone had the right to criticize me, it was Winston. It is safe to say that Winston's self-esteem was healthy, and he had no need to try to feel better about himself by diminishing someone else. He could freely affirm me. When he did, he gave back to me what the others had tried to take away—my right to choose what was best for me, my right to be myself.

I needed Winston's affirmation. I was strong enough that I'd have been all right without it, but the others had hurt me. I needed someone to help heal the wound. And Winston's affirmation did something else for me. In telling me to feel okay, he helped restore the joy and excitement I'd felt about having a car I knew I deserved. I felt renewed strength. In a sense my selfhood "cleared up." The others might continue to tease me, but I would feel joy even in the midst of opposition, and I would not feel shame about my decision or false guilt about buying a car.

LEARNING TO FOCUS

We are born with the ability to discover and know who we are. The true source of our identities lies at the fingertips of our own consciousness. As our awareness of ourselves, our families, and our world grows, affirmation is the most important ingredient in the process of learning to know ourselves. Only human violation, false guilt, and destructive shame prevent our discovering who we are. Nothing else can interfere and cause us confusion about our identities.

Throughout history many have tried to invent other ways of discovering inner personal identities by using gimmicks or mysterious "forces," even so-called superpowers, to discover their true selves. Different philosophies, religions, and cults have been developed for the sake of higher consciousness. Many people use drugs to heighten awareness. But we don't need these methods to know who we are.

The power to know ourselves is within us. God gave us this potential when He gave us the gift of human consciousness. There is no higher form of human awareness. We need God to direct us through life and free our minds from true guilt, but we don't need metaphysics to find ourselves. We only need to be free of psychological guilt and destructive shame and to give ourselves permission to feel worthy. The potential is in us to learn to simply say, "This is me," and to be fully aware of our needs, wants, desires, and idiosyncrasies. We must recapture this potential, and we can do it without violating others.

At times God wants and allows us to fulfill our needs; at other times He chooses to have us deny our needs. It does not get much more complicated than that. But if we can't focus, we can't know ourselves, and we are at the mercy of the mysterious, the fortune tellers, the stargazers, and the wishes of others.

Because of the complexity of the world, in order to take care of ourselves we need to have the freedom, power, and authority to make our own choices. We are fools if we don't demand that freedom, for when we don't we give away our identities to others. False guilt creeps in. Because of our intense need for acceptance, every time a person or society tells us how we should be, our minds begin to drift. The conscious parts of our minds move away from our selfhoods and focus on the demands of the world. But such focusing requires us to create a mental fog to take our selfhoods out of focus. When we can't focus on our own selfhoods, we can't be responsible for ourselves, and we are at the mercy of the world.

One of the most unfortunate aspects of our culture is that we start out all too willing to affirm a newborn child's uniqueness and creativity, only to squash this same person later as he develops his unique identity. When the child is young, we feel free to affirm him without hesitation. We are amused with his silliness, his spontaneity, and his off-the-wall remarks. We enjoy the ways he is different from other children. But when that child begins to grow up, stretch his talents, challenge our values, and compete with us, his identity begins to threaten us. As he grows and develops, we—as parents, as a society, and often as a church—find it necessary to imprison him in our opinions of who and what he should become. When we do that, we give him the message that he's not okay. We take from him the corner-stone of his own selfhood, the right to be okay with himself.

I once counseled Sharon, a woman who smeared her lipstick, partially missing her lips as she applied it. She had been diagnosed as a schizophrenic, and I just accepted this as part of her crazy behavior. After a few months in therapy, however, I realized that Sharon was doing quite well with applying her lipstick, as well as the rest of her makeup. Curious, I asked her why she smeared her lipstick. She told me that it had been impossible for her to look at herself in a mirror until recently. When she tried, all she could see was a blur. She learned to apply her lipstick without looking at her face.

Why was it so hard for Sharon to look at herself? When she was a child her mother constantly told her she was ugly. All this criticism made her feel ugly. With these feelings of ugliness came a deeper fear that she really was an ugly person. She did not have the ego strength to look at herself and feel okay about herself regardless of what others thought. She dared not take a chance that they were wrong. Subconsciously she had to literally blur her vision.

I believe that to a degree Sharon is typical of all of us. She didn't blur her vision only to avoid seeing her face. She was afraid to see all of herself. She had many talents, but she hid them behind her fear. She couldn't focus on them and maximize what God had given her.

We all have talents that we hide with the fear of not being good enough. In a sense, like Sharon, we're afraid we are really ugly. The world chooses which gifts and talents are most honored, and if we don't possess these super gifts we feel inadequate. We blur our vision, the lenses of our real potentials.

When we develop the ability to focus on what God has given us, we learn to use these talents not only to serve ourselves, but more importantly to serve mankind. When we take what we have, affirm it, and maximize it, we allow ourselves to feel the deepest sense of worth.

FREEDOM TO BE OURSELVES

I like neatness and order. Consequently, sometimes I have been critical of people whose homes were messy or disorganized. I believed that having a messy home was wrong until I counseled Brenda, a woman who had spent a good part of her childhood locked in a closet.

Brenda's mother did not just lock her in the closet. To punish her more severely, she put this child in there naked, without blankets or clothing to keep her warm or toys to play with. Brenda endured long, cold hours of total isolation with nothing to hold onto for security. As an adult Brenda needed clutter around her, because it brought her a sense of security. Consequently, she preferred a messy, cluttered house.

Brenda's need for clutter made me realize that I feel more secure when I have everything neatly in place. The mistake I had made was believing my way of feeling secure was somehow more "godly" than ways that are different.

We often make this mistake. Instead of simply loving others with a sense of our own internal security, we approach them burdened by our fears. Then to cover up those fears, we incorporate a set of self-righteous values to judge them by.

Granted, a messy or dirty house is sometimes irresponsible or insensitive. But needing to be overly neat and structured, with everything in life in its proper order and place, can also be the result of insensitivity to others who may not choose to be that way.

If you really think someone's behavior is out of line and causing him harm or harming someone else, you should confront him in love. But few of us take the courage to confront. We would rather judge. When we judge someone, we tell that person he does not have the right to be the way he is, and we give ourselves permission to play God in the lives of others.

Every little unfair judgment takes away a portion of an individual's ability and right to focus on himself. Yes, we each have the right to focus on ourselves. We have the right to be ourselves. We have the right to affirm our idiosyncrasies and to be different. We have the right to choose our own paths in life independently of the wishes of others. Certainly we can't be so self-centered that we become totally insensitive to God's will and the needs and wishes of others. But real motivation to reach our potential and genuine love for others must begin with our own uniqueness and gifts.

About fifteen years ago, during one of the lowest points of my life, Peb Jackson invited me to go rock climbing with him and his friend, Tim Hansel. Tim operated an outdoor adventure organization, and Peb was on the board of directors.

I was unaware of how low my self-esteem was at that time and completely unprepared for the blessing the pure acceptance of these two men would be. Both of them are masters at affirming people. I clearly remember that first day with Peb and Tim when I set out to learn the art of rock climbing.

I grew up in a semi-country environment and I had

some natural ability, so it was easy for me to pick up the techniques. Every time I made a good move on a rock, they were quick to praise me. When I got stuck, which happened many times, they were right there to help me get unstuck. Not once did they judge me, and I will never forget just how good their encouragement felt. This unconditional acceptance of my personhood helped me rediscover myself and bring it out of the fog of my subconscious.

When the personhood is hidden in the subconscious we rediscover it by affirming ourselves and cultivating relationships with people who affirm us, the way Peb and Tim affirmed me.

How do you discover your personhood? Remember, you never lost it. It is hidden in the fog of your subconscious. You've lost sight of parts of it because those parts are too painful to look at. To recapture these parts, you need to exercise your freedom to make your own decisions and determine what is right for you. And remember, you also need outside sources of affirmation to help you.

Discovering your true identity is not simply the process of discovering who you are from an existential standpoint. It is the affirmation and enjoyment of who you already are—what God has already created in you. For example, working through the shamed part of your sexual identity to a full and proper affirmation of this part of your selfhood is a way to discover your true identity. Working through the shame and guilt that might be preventing a full and joyful relationship with

God and others is another important way to know who you are. Shame forces you to focus off what God created in you and to chase the philosophies of the world.

GOD'S UNCONDITIONAL AFFIRMATION

Jesus himself so beautifully affirmed the person. He spent time with the leper and the immoral tax collector. He allowed a prostitute to pour ointment on his feet. Yet He never wavered from confronting a person with love about sinful behavior. When confronting the religious leaders of the day who were about to stone an adulterous woman to death, He did not attack their personhoods or try to shame them. He simply said, "He who is without sin among you, let him throw a stone at her first" (John 8:7).

When Jesus sat above Jerusalem, He wept for the people there. He loved each individual, yet He could see how they were destroying each other's beautiful personhoods with their sinful, violating natures.

I believe that parents and the church share the major responsibility for helping a lost world to find itself. Parents can give their children that gift by learning how to affirm each child's individuality, just as the church needs to receive and affirm every person who seeks God there.

The church needs to work harder to clarify and separate the different kinds of guilt and shame, which separate the affirmation of the person from the disaffirmation of his sinful or irresponsible behavior. Churches seem to swing from one extreme to the other.

Either there is an over-affirmation of the total person, without any acknowledgment of a person's sinful side, or the total person is condemned as sinful. Over-affirmation tends to encourage loose moral standards. Total condemnation of the person causes the individual to lose his or her sense of self and the church will likely begin to over-control him.

Our churches and our homes should be the safest places in the world for our tender personalities. Cleansed of our sins by the work of Christ, we should be free to affirm the person. Our churches and our homes should be our sanctuaries where we find unconditional love. Unfortunately often they aren't. Instead of unconditional love and healing, we experience humans who are judgmental according to the self-righteous or wrong values they have invented to hide their own fears. As they try to impose their values on us and tell us who and what we should be, we feel guilt until we are so bound by it we can't stop being judgmental toward ourselves and others.

Others whose self-esteem and identities are clouded by self-doubt, fear, guilt, and shame try daily to violate you. They are unable to give you unconditional love and affirmation. The constant hammering can cause you to be confused about your identity and value as a person. Like Sharon, your mind may blur your vision of yourself.

You need to recapture the ability to focus on your own selfhood. What more valuable goal could you have than to love yourself and be responsible for yourself?

When you take on this task, you will become more useful to God and the world.

Does this mean that you should spend your whole life in introspection? No. Your goal should be to have the ability, when necessary, to focus inward to properly take care of your own personhood. Unhealed or undernourished selves constantly need attention. But when your personhood has been properly nourished and affirmed, you will be free to give to the world in the most unconditional way possible.

Your selfhood is something very special. It is *you*. God wants you to search for it. He wants to take your individual selfhood and use it for your joy and His glory. That is your ultimate purpose. The You that God created will be fully known by you and fully used by God. Then you, the person, will be fully alive and fully at peace with yourself.

Some Additional Help

GUILT WORK SHEETS

To help you master the guilt in your life, I have developed a Guilt Work Sheet. You will find several copies in Appendix B. The first two sheets are filled out using the two examples in Chapter Three. I suggest you use these work sheets with a few examples from your own life until you have mastered the concepts for recognizing and eliminating true and false guilt.

Shame is often much more difficult to master because it involves a healing process. This process takes time because it requires gradually lifting up wounded parts from your subconscious. As you begin the healing process, thus strengthening your self-esteem, more parts will begin to emerge that need to be healed.

ADDITIONAL READING MATERIALS

For further help with healing your shame, several books are available. I especially recommend *Healing the Shame That Binds You* by John Bradshaw, published by Health Communications, Inc., Deerfield Beach, Florida, and *Letting Go of Shame* by Ronald and Patricia Potter-Efron, published by Hazelden Educational Materials of Center City, Minnesota. These books include a variety of exercises. Read both of them and choose the exercises that seem to best fit your particular needs.

Because of the nature of shame, the exercises in these two books are quite good. Shame covers the wounded areas of our inner selves, the parts that have been made unlovable by violations. You might be somewhat aware of these areas in your own self, but your denial system will do its best to hide these areas from you. Consequently, you may be more aware of a general feeling of shame than of the specific wounded areas.

For example, a person may feel bad or shameful about his or her sexuality, wage earning potential, body image, or relationship to the opposite sex. This general feeling of badness represents specific wounds. Specific events caused the wounds. A specific abusive event, a specific way a parent belittled you, or a specific way your peers teased you is responsible for a particular wound to your selfhood.

For healing to take place, the specifically wounded area needs to be known and felt. In other words, if you feel bad about yourself, you can't just go to a seminar or a therapist and heal your "generalized" sense of badness. The exercises in the Bradshaw and Potter-Efron books will help you spell out exactly what happened to you or what you do to yourself to cause the shame.

A WORD OF CAUTION

These exercises are a way for you to take the first step—the awareness step. Your shamed parts will still need to be interfaced with an outside source of love or affirmation. Sharing these bruised parts with a therapist, a support group, or your loved ones will help to replace the coldness and emptiness of the wound with felt inner warmth.

As I shared before, in my younger years I feared writing. Once I started writing, I forgot all about that wounded part. I just assumed it was healed, so I never tried to share it with anyone. Maybe I still felt too ashamed to do that.

In the process of writing this book, I shared this wounded part for the first time. I was surprised when I wrote down this episode of my life for you to read. I felt a healing taking place. I let this wounded part up to the surface for the first time. More importantly, I knew that you would accept this part of me. Even though I don't know you personally, your love helped to heal this wound.

Use the Guilt Work Sheets to help identify false guilt and remove it from your life. Identify the areas of yourself that were wounded or shamed in the past and let them up to be healed. If these areas are dangerously large, causing you to feel emotionally unstable, seek professional help. I also encourage you to seek a support group, possibly a Twelve-Step program, to help heal your shame. If your shame is the result of significant wounds, you will most likely need the more individualized help of a professional therapist. When seeking professional help, make certain your therapist is a feeling oriented therapist who has experience working with people from abused or dysfunctional pasts.

And please, don't be too rough on yourself if you can't make the material in this book work immediately. Remember: no more guilt. Work the book. Share this book and what you are learning with others. Ask for their feedback. Let the process and the awareness gradually and naturally unfold for you.

Good luck and God bless.

Steps to Eliminate Guilt

Step 1. *Recognize the guilt and stop your mind—don't allow yourself to draw quick conclusions.*

Step 2. *Identify the real source of the guilt or pain.*

Step 3. *Determine whether you are feeling true guilt or false guilt.*

Step 4. *If it is true guilt:*
   a. Confess it.
   b. Ask forgiveness.
   c. Change your irresponsible behavior.
   d. Forgive yourself and move on.

Step 5. *If it is false guilt:*
   a. Reverse the emotional process from false guilt to a little anger.

b. Feel and release the hurt.
c. Confront and/or correct the violating situation when necessary and possible.

Guilt Work Sheet

Situation or event: *Voting incident with George*

Step 1. RECOGNITION: When and where did I first notice guilt?
> *When I was by myself, I felt some shame or guilt.*

Step 2. SOURCE: What incident(s) precipitated the event?
> *When George put me down for not voting.*

Step 3. TRUE OR FALSE GUILT: Did I intentionally or irresponsibly do anything?
> *No.*

Step 4. TRUE GUILT: What do I need to do to correct the true guilt? (confess it, ask forgiveness, change my behavior)
  Nothing.

Step 5. FALSE GUILT: What do I need to do to eliminate the false guilt?
  a) Do I feel a little anger?
     Yes, once I realized the source of the pain. To myself, I said, "That George, he got me again."

  b) Am I able to feel and release some pain?
     Yes, I could feel the hurt that he caused.

  c) Do I need to confront or correct the situation?
     No, not unless he keeps this behavior up.

  d) Am I still feeling some guilt and/or shame and do I need some outside help with this situation?
     No.

Guilt Work Sheet

Situation or event: *Melissa's guilt from moving*

Step 1. RECOGNITION: When and where did I first notice guilt?
Every time I talk with my mother.

Step 2. SOURCE: What incident(s) precipitated the event?
My mother and more precisely my moving.

Step 3. TRUE OR FALSE GUILT: Did I intentionally or irresponsibly do anything?
No, I did not intentionally want to hurt my mother.

Step 4. TRUE GUILT: What do I need to do to correct the true guilt? (confess it, ask forgiveness, change my behavior)

Nothing.

Step 5. FALSE GUILT: What do I need to do to eliminate the false guilt?

    a) Do I feel a little anger?

    Hard. I am just starting to but I feel guilty for even feeling some anger.

    b) Am I able to feel and release some pain?

    Yes. As I share how much my mother has controlled me, I feel the pain.

    c) Do I need to confront or correct the situation?

    Yes. I need to set limits with my mother.

    d) Am I still feeling some guilt and/or shame and do I need some outside help with this situation?

    I need to stay in therapy until I am strong enough to set proper boundaries with my mother and other persons.

Guilt Work Sheet

Situation or event: _____

Step 1. RECOGNITION: When and where did I first notice guilt?

Step 2. SOURCE: What incident(s) precipitated the event?

Step 3. TRUE OR FALSE GUILT: Did I intentionally or irresponsibly do anything?

Step 4. TRUE GUILT: What do I need to do to correct the true guilt? (confess it, ask forgiveness, change my behavior)

Step 5. FALSE GUILT: What do I need to do to eliminate the false guilt?
   a) Do I feel a little anger?

   b) Am I able to feel and release some pain?

   c) Do I need to confront or correct the situation?

   d) Am I still feeling some guilt and/or shame and do I need some outside help with this situation?

Guilt Work Sheet

Situation or event: _____

Step 1. RECOGNITION: When and where did I first notice guilt?

Step 2. SOURCE: What incident(s) precipitated the event?

Step 3. TRUE OR FALSE GUILT: Did I intentionally or irresponsibly do anything?

Step 4. TRUE GUILT: What do I need to do to correct the true guilt? (confess it, ask forgiveness, change my behavior)

Step 5. FALSE GUILT: What do I need to do to eliminate the false guilt?

a) Do I feel a little anger?

b) Am I able to feel and release some pain?

c) Do I need to confront or correct the situation?

d) Am I still feeling some guilt and/or shame and do I need some outside help with this situation?

About the Author

Ty C. Colbert is a licensed clinical psychologist and a senior staff member of the Adult Children Centers in Orange, California. His practice specializes in treating issues of anger and guilt, adults of dysfunctional families, marital problems, co-dependency, depression, and sexual abuse.

Dr. Colbert holds the M.A. from Pepperdine University and the Ph.D. in counseling psychology from the University of Southern California. He lives in Santa Ana, California, with his family.